What people are saying about this book...

"WOW! This is the clearest and most complete book on knowing the will of God I have ever seen."

   - Pastor Randy Casey, Ketha Heights Baptist Church

"This book changed my life... I couldn't stop reading it... Amazingly, things on my list of things to do, are now not mine, but His, and they get done! I walk with the Lord all day... My days are now full of peace... I feel His presence, I feel His love..."

   - Richard Dinker, Kona, Hawaii

"I love this book. I want our whole congregation to read it. I felt like it summarized years of the messages God has given to me as I have taught through the scriptures, verse by verse. And the book said it so well...It gave me insight into His Word that I had not seen before... This book needed to be written."

   - Pastor Henry Gainey, Calvary Chapel Thomasville

"This book really gets into the nuts and bolts of discerning God's will. It tackles the topic with simplicity and practicality and it is presented in a way that the reader can really get their mind around it, and their hands on it."

   - Pastor J.D. Farag, Calvary Chapel Kaneohe

How to Know the Will of God

Living a Life of Knowing God's Will, Right Decision Making, and Intimacy with God

Strat Goodhue

First Call Publishing
Haiku, Hawaii

How to Know the Will of God

Living a Life of Knowing God's Will, Right Decision Making, and Intimacy with God

First Call Publishing
Post Office Box 81459
Haiku, HI 96708

contact@firstcallpublishing.org   www.firstcallpublishing.org

Library of Congress Control Number: 2012946157

ISBN: 978-0-9858418-0-5

Contents

ACKNOWLEDGMENTS

First and foremost, I would like to thank God. It has been such a blessing writing and working on this book, knowing that God can use even me, to bless some of His children. It is a privilege I could never deserve.

I am also grateful for my wonderful wife, Doreen. She not only helped make this a better book, she helped me to experience joy as I wrote it.

I want to express my special appreciation for Pastor Tim Newman at Calvary Chapel Windward. He has been a wonderful pastor, friend, neighbor, landlord, boss, and brother-in-law over the years. His love for God's Word is a blessing to many.

I would like to express my deep gratitude for Charlie Cook, Paul and Geri Ely, and many others whose prayers, encouragement and support for Doreen and I have been such a big part of this book being written.

I would also like to thank Sally Richardson, who helped with the editing. She is a precious sister in the Lord, and a good friend.

Lastly, I offer my sincere appreciation to those of you who will read this book, and I pray, be blessed by it.

Introduction

"It's wonderful to do the Lord's work, but it is greater still to do the Lord's will." - Miriam Booth

Have you ever gotten to the end of a day and wondered, "Did I do God's will today, or my will? Was I being led by God, or by my own thoughts? How can I tell the difference?" One of the questions most commonly asked by Christians is "How can I know God's will?" When you ask people about it, they will usually say something about praying and reading the Bible. While the answer is rich with truth, it sounds so simple. You can't help but wonder if somehow there may be a bit more to it. "I read my Bible. I pray. Why don't I know whether or not God is really leading my life? Should I just assume that He is?" Whether you are a new Christian or have known the Lord for decades, these are questions we can all wonder about.

What is worth more than all of the riches in the world? Peace of mind- Not just a passing feeling of peacefulness, but a deep, lasting peace; a sense of safety and a sure confidence in the future. And there is nothing that will produce more peace of mind than having an intimate relationship with God, knowing that you are in the center of His will, and that He is directing your life. The purpose of this book is not only to help you in discovering God's will for the big decisions in life, but also to help you to live a life of knowing God's will.

Wouldn't it be nice if every morning when you woke up, there was a hand written note from God on the nightstand next to your bed that said something along the lines of "Dear (your name here), I love you very much and My plans for you are wonderful. Here is a list of great things I have for you today... Love, God" and wouldn't it be nice if God spoke to you in a loud and clear, audible voice all day long? He could tell you the wisest and best things to do and say in every situation. You would never make a mistake. Well, as we know, that's not how God guides us. God knows that leaving daily notes on our nightstands and texting us on our cell phones are not the best ways to guide us into His will.

How important is it that we know and do His will? Jesus said "Not everyone who says to Me, 'Lord, Lord' shall enter the Kingdom of Heaven, but he who does the will of My Father who is in Heaven."[1] This verse and others like it make it very clear that it is vital for us to seek to do God's will. Are any of us going to perform God's will perfectly? No. We all fall short,[2] but it should be our aim to follow God's plans for our life.

In the book of Proverbs we are told, "Trust in the Lord with all your heart and lean not on your own understanding. In all your ways acknowledge Him, and He shall direct your paths."[3] If we are making decisions by "leaning on" our own understanding, we are not

---

[1] Matthew 7:21
[2] Romans 3:23
[3] Proverbs 3:5-6

following God's direction.[4] How much of the time do we miss God's "good and acceptable and perfect"[5] will for our lives because we are living day after day being led by our own thinking rather than truly trusting in Him and acknowledging Him?

We can be freed from our natural tendency to lean on our own understanding and in this book, we will be exploring how to do that. By learning how to follow God's leading, we can walk in the path that God has for us- a path of freedom and joy.

God's will is not something that only a few "super spiritual" people have access to. It is something that God wants every one of us to know and to walk in every day. In fact, God wants to guide us more than we want to be guided.

It is my hope that you will find gems in this book that will change your life and that this book will help you to obtain something worth more than all the wealth in the world- that rich life of joy and fruitfulness that only comes from an intimate relationship with the loving God. It is also my hope that you will know God's will for your life, not just in the big decisions, but all day, every day.

---

[4] The admonition is to not "lean on" our understanding. It is not telling us however, that we should not "use" our understanding. We are commanded to love the Lord with all of our mind (Matthew 22:37, Mark 12:30, Luke 10:27), so following the Lord definitely involves the use of our minds. The distinction between the two will be discussed later in the book.

[5] Romans 12:2

1

Knowing the Will of God

"...the one who does the will of God lives forever."
-1 John 2:17

Feeling out of touch with God

We want to do what God wants us to do but we don't always know what that is. How do we know God's will? Sometimes we end up guessing at it and kind of "winging it," hoping that we are getting it right. Even though we pray to God, we can feel like we aren't really very close to Him. It can be frustrating. We make unwise decisions and end up in trouble. God is there to help us out of the messes we get ourselves into but we can't help thinking that there has got to be a better way to go through life. There is.

Our life can be radically changed, and it can change so quickly that we will be amazed. Our spiritual life can go from dry and monotonous, to a life that is spiritually productive and filled with joy. In addition to that, our life will truly please and glorify God. What a wonderful thing that is- you can live a life that pleases the Creator of the universe.

Do you want your life to be abundant?

Jesus said, "I have come that they may have life, and that they may have it more abundantly."[1] We can go through life not living the abundant life God wants for us, or we can make a life-changing decision. What is this decision and what is this going to cost you? Well, you must decide to do whatever is necessary for you to hear clearly from God, and you must be willing to do what He will tell you to do. The rewards are not only out of this world (in Heaven) but are rich here on earth. They may not come in the form of material possessions and wealth, but the value of them will far surpass anything money can buy; a life that pleases God and brings you a deep joy and intimacy with Him. It is a life that is filled with the satisfaction that comes from knowing that you are doing what God wants you to do and being who God wants you to be. You can also have confidence that at the end of this life, you will stand before the King of the universe and He will say to you, something along the lines of, "Well done, good and faithful servant; you have been faithful over a few things, I will make you ruler over many things. Enter into the joy of your Lord."[2]

> "I have come that they may have life, and that they may have it more abundantly."
> - John 10:10

Have you ever thought about what it would be like to have the Creator of the universe speak those words

---

[1] John 10:10
[2] Matthew 25:23

of praise to you? To hear God Himself say, "Well done," and to call you "good and faithful" and then to tell you to enter into His joy? Wow! What must that joy be like? It will be a joy more rewarding and fulfilling than anything that could be found in this world. As the Psalmist wrote, "In Your presence, there is fullness of joy; At Your right hand are pleasures forevermore."[3] Forever is a long time (it never ends) and to experience His joy and pleasure forever is going to be fantastic beyond our wildest dreams.

Are you afraid of the will of God?

It's a worry that can resurface over and over in our lives, "If I totally surrender to the will of God, He is going to make me do things I hate doing and go places I don't want to go. I will end up lonely and suffering in ways that most people never have to experience. I will be… miserable." You probably haven't thought about it in those exact words but you get the idea.

> Some people worry that if they fully surrender to God and His will, they will end up miserable.

We worry that if we surrender completely to God and His will, we will end up miserable. We think that maybe God's plans for us are bad and that He will want us to do the one thing we most hate to do- as though God was a big ogre in the sky who is looking for ways to make our lives difficult.

---

[3] Psalm 16:11

Why do we think like that? Because we really don't know God very well. We think that we couldn't possibly live a satisfied life if we surrenedered to God, but as J. Hudson Taylor, the great missionary to China, wrote, "The real secret of an unsatisfied life lies too often in an unsurrendered will."[4]

King David said, "How precious also are Your thoughts to me, O God! How great is the sum of them! If I should count them, they would be more in number than the sand."[5] Have you ever picked up a handful of sand and tried to count the number of grains? There are thousands of grains of sand in a spoonful, about a hundred thousand in a handful. I heard that someone calculated that there are seven quintillion, five hundred quadrillion (7,500,000,000,000,000,000) grains of sand on the beaches of the world. That's only the beaches. If you were to add in all the sand in the deserts of the world, you'd end up with a much bigger number.

> "The real secret of an unsatisfied life lies too often in an unsurrendered will."
> - J. Hudson Taylor

Do you think that God thought that much about King David but doesn't really care about you? The Bible tells us that "God is love."[6] It doesn't just say that He is sort of loving. No, the Bible says that God *is* love. Love is one of His chief attributes. It's His character. It's who

---

[4] Taylor, James Hudson. Union And Communion or Thoughts on the Song of Solomon (p. 4). Public Domain Books. Kindle Edition.
[5] Psalm 139:18
[6] 1 John 4:16

He is. As the Apostle Paul said, "He who did not spare His own Son, but delivered Him up for us all, how shall He not with Him also freely give us all things?"[7]

Do you know two or three people who you think, really know God well? Maybe people who have been walking with God for many years? Ask them to tell you the most important truths they have learned about God. They probably won't say anything about God wanting their life to be hard, or that he expects too much. Their answer will probably be something about God's love, His faithfulness, His mercy or His grace (undeserved kindness). The more you get to know God, the more you will realize how much He loves you.

God loves His children more than any person on earth has ever loved their child. Does that mean that God

> The more you get to know God, the more you will realize how much He loves you.

wants us to live a life of ease without ever having difficulties of any kind? Any parent who loves their child wants what's best for their child. They don't want them to suffer needlessly, but at the same time, they know that in order to mature, a child must face difficulties. Everything God wants for us is for good. At times it's extremely difficult and sometimes we don't understand why God is allowing us to go through difficulties and suffering, but "all things work together for good to those who love God."[8] Sometimes years pass before we realize why God has allowed us to

---

[7] Romans 8:32
[8] Romans 8:28

endure a certain trial in our life. In some cases, we may not find out the reasons until we get to Heaven. But then we will see clearly[9] and we will see how perfect our Heavenly Father is and how perfect His plans for us are. As the prophet Micah said, "He delights in unchanging love."[10] There is absolutely no reason to fear God's will for your life. (We'll explore this further in the next chapter.)

Walking in the light

We can make a few changes and have a life of peace and joy. Not that we won't have hard times. Jesus said that we would have them,[11] but we can have joy, a peace that passes understanding, and we can know God's will for our life. God's will is not supposed to be a mystery. God, through the Apostle Paul, even commanded us to "understand what the Lord's will is."[12]

Even though we can't physically see God, and we walk by faith, not by sight[13], our Christian walk is not supposed to be like someone who is blindly walking in the dark. It is supposed to be a walk in the light. As Jesus said, "My sheep hear My voice, and I know them, and they follow Me."[14] The picture Jesus gives to us is of sheep following a Shepherd. Sheep don't follow their shepherd at a great distance, walking along blindly

---

[9] 1 Corinthians 13:12
[10] Micah 7:18
[11] John 16:33
[12] Ephesians 5:17
[13] 2Corinthians 5:7
[14] John 10:27

bumping into rocks and walls, guessing until they figure out which way their shepherd wants them to go. On the other hand, they aren't given a detailed map to follow either. They simply stay close to, and follow the voice of the one they've learned to follow- their shepherd. How do we get to know the Great Shepherd's voice? Just like a sheep with its shepherd, we learn what His voice sounds like by hearing it repeatedly, over time. As we will explore in this book, it is something we can definitely learn to recognize through experience as we choose to follow our loving Shepherd.

Knowing God and His will

It is an amazing truth that the Creator of the universe, who knows the beginning and the end, desires for us to know Him intimately and to be guided by Him. Jesus said that eternal life consists of knowing both our Heavenly Father and Jesus Christ.[15] The word "know" (in John 17:3) in the original language does not simply mean to know about something, or to know that a certain thing is true; like we know that Abraham Lincoln was one of the U.S. Presidents. The word implies knowledge based on personal experience. It's the same word used by Jesus when He said, "As the Father knows Me, even so I know the Father."[16] Jesus is telling us that we can know God personally, not just believe in Him like some people believe in the tooth fairy or Santa Claus.

---

[15] John 17:3
[16] John 10:15

Knowing God is at the heart of the Christian life. God should not be the way to get everything we want; as much as God should be everything we want. He is not just a means to an end, He is the end. He is the goal. He is the prize.

> Knowing God is at the heart of the Christian life. God should not be the way to get everything we want; as much as God should be everything we want. He is not just a means to an end, He is the end.

This is a basic truth of Christianity and it is also a key to knowing God's will. As we seek to know God more intimately, we will become more adept at knowing His will. At the same time, as we seek to know God's will, we will find ourselves knowing God in a deeper way.

He cares deeply about us and He wants to guide us into the absolute best for our lives. As He says to us in the book of Psalms, "I will instruct you and teach you in the way you should go; I will guide you with My eye. Do not be like the horse or like the mule, which have no understanding, which must be harnessed with bit and bridle…"[17] He wants to guide us with His "eye." In other words, He wants us to be so sensitive to His leading, that when He intends for us to go in a certain direction, we will know it. As the Apostle Paul prayed for the Christians in the city of Colossae, God's desire is that we would "be filled with the knowledge of His

---

[17] Psalm 32:8-9

will."[18] God wants you to know His will more than you want to know His will.

Microwave oven Christianity

In the U.S., we live in a microwave oven culture. We put a plate of food in a microwave oven and we push a button. We wait a few seconds and then we grow impatient. "Is this food ever going to get hot?" In many villages around the world, just getting water to drink every day may require a half-hour hike or more, but when we Americans want something, we want it now!

> God wants you to know His will more than you want to know His will.

We want to know God's will instantly (and it's great that sometimes we can). We want the formula, but the will of God is not found in a formula. It is found in a person- the person of Jesus Christ. The Apostle Peter said "...His divine power has given to us all things that pertain to life and godliness, through the knowledge of Him. . ."[19] Jesus commanded us to follow Him, not to follow a 3 step plan to success. Following Jesus is a step by step walk. That having been said, there are ways that God chooses to communicate with us, and if we know what those ways are, we can

> We want the formula, but the will of God is not found in a formula. It is found in a person- the person of Jesus Christ.

---

[18] Colossians 1:9
[19] 2 Peter 1:2-3

quickly learn to discern His will in ways that some might spend years, decades or even a whole lifetime learning. You can live an abundant life- a life of walking in the light and knowing God's will.

Heavenly Father, Thank you for being such a wonderful God. Please give me abundant life- a life of walking with You and knowing You. I want my life to be filled with Your peace and joy. Help me to be open to making any changes in my life that will help me to better hear Your voice and to follow You more closely. In Jesus' name I pray, Amen.

2

It Starts at the Cross

"I delight to do Your will, O my God..."

-Psalm 40:8

I hate missing the beginning of a movie. You know how it is. You walk into the movie theater late, or you turn on the television after a movie has started and you have to try to figure out what has already happened. Sometimes you never really figure it out. For certain movies, if you don't see the beginning, you won't get it. Knowing the will of God is kind of like that. You need to start at the beginning.

Getting to know God and His will for us, starts at the cross. What does that mean? God is absolutely Perfect, Righteous, and Holy. Sin causes a separation between us and God. Because God is perfectly Good and a God of absolute justice, a penalty needs to be paid for every sin. Jesus died on the cross to pay the penalty of our sins, and to reconcile us to God.

There would be no relationship with God and no walking in His will, if it weren't for Jesus dying on the cross. Jesus is "the way"[1] to God.

---

[1] John 14:6

Motivation for doing the will of God

Not only is knowing God's will made possible through the cross, but the motivation to do God's will comes through the cross as well. "God loves you so much that He sent His only begotten Son to die for you." We may have heard that a hundred or even thousands of times. The reason that we decided to put our faith in Jesus is probably because we heard that good news, and yet the truth of that statement may only be another statement of fact to us now. "Yes, I know that Jesus died for me. I know that God loves me. That's why I'm a Christian." We may not be any more passionate about that statement than we would be about the statement, "The refrigerator is in the kitchen." Does

> God loves you. That is a radically life-changing truth for you to realize.

the fact that there is a refrigerator in your kitchen affect you on a daily basis? Yes, but it's probably not something that you marvel at, or think much about. The love of God however, is something worth thinking about and marveling at. God loves you. That is a radically life-changing truth for you to realize.

God really loves you

For some of us, that statement may make us a little bit uncomfortable. We know ourselves (and our short-comings) too well. We might believe that God loves us to some degree, but not be comfortable with the statement "God really loves me." It can be a hard thing for us to accept- The God who created the universe, the heavens and the earth, loves us as individuals. It is true that He is absolutely Holy, all-powerful, all-knowing, and absolutely Righteous, and it is also true that He loves you. Until you have that fact planted in your mind and heart, your Christian life will never be abundant. You can go to church, read your Bible, try to do good things, serve the Lord and maybe even become a leader in the church,

> "We love Him because He first loved us." - 1 John 4:19

but there will always be a bit of emptiness, a sense of lack of fulfillment. You may feel like you aren't doing enough. Do you sometimes wonder if you are really a Christian? Even though there came a point in your life when you turned from your sins as best you knew how and received Jesus as your Lord and Savior, you may still feel like there's something you haven't done to really be a Christian.

The problem may be a matter of emphasis. The crux of the matter for us as people who have sinned and fall short of the glory of God,[2] is not what we do to be good enough for God; *it is what He has already done for us.* Jesus suffered and died on the cross to pay the penalty for your sins. Why? Because God is merciful and He loves you. That's a vital thing for you to know. Pray about it. Ask the Lord to help you to know how much He loves you. You need to know on a deep level that God loves you. Why? Because our motivation for walking with God, the reason we want to know His will and do what He wants us to do, should be our love for Him. As the Apostle John said, "We love Him because

---

[2] Romans 3:23

He first loved us."[3] This is critical. The highest motivation we can have in life is love for God, inspired by His love for us. This love for God is not something we can work up in our own strength. We can't force ourselves to love God.

Jesus told a parable about a religious leader and a tax collector. He said "Two men went up to the temple to pray, one a Pharisee and the other a tax collector. The Pharisee stood and prayed thus with himself, 'God, I thank You that I am not like other men--extortioners, unjust, adulterers, or even as this tax collector. I fast twice a week; I give tithes of all that I possess.' And the tax collector, standing afar off, would not so much as raise his eyes to heaven, but beat his breast, saying, 'God, be merciful to me a sinner!' I tell you, this man went down to his house justified rather than the other;"[4] Jesus was illustrating the point that we all need the forgiveness of God. As the Apostle Paul said, "There is none righteous, no, not one."[5]

God solves our problem

Do you think that you have sinned a little or a lot in your life? If you think you've only sinned a little, you're mistaken. If we look at our lives compared to the standard of God's Holy Law, the Ten Commandments, we will quickly realize that each of us is guilty of falling far short of true goodness. Have you always loved God more than anything else? Have you ever lied? The Bible

---

[3] 1st John 4:19
[4] Luke 18:10-14
[5] Romans 3:10

says all liars deserve to be in the lake of fire.[6] Have you ever stolen anything (no matter how small)? Have you ever used God's name in vain (using the name of the God who created you in place of a filthy word)? Have you ever said or done anything that was disrespectful toward your parents? Have you ever had feelings of lust for someone that wasn't your spouse? If you have, then according to Jesus you have committed adultery in your heart.[7] Have you ever been angry at someone without a perfectly good reason? If so, then according to Jesus, it's as if you have committed murder in your heart.[8]

We don't need to look at all of the Ten Commandments to see that we are guilty of breaking God's Laws.[9] We are all going to stand before God on Judgment day,[10] and if we are trusting in our own goodness, we will be in a dire situation indeed. We need God's mercy.

In 1773, John Newton penned the words of the well known hymn, Amazing Grace. The hymn starts with the words "Amazing Grace, how sweet the sound, that saved a wretch like me. I once was lost but now am found, was blind, but now I see." If you think the words "a wretch like me," in no way could describe you, then there's something you really don't understand about God's holiness or about your own sinfulness (or both).

---

[6] Revelation 21:8
[7] Matthew 5:28
[8] Matthew 5:21-22
[9] Romans 3:23
[10] Hebrews 9:27

Surely, we are sinful creatures and truly, God is a merciful and gracious God.

Some people think that since God is good and loving, that at the end of their life when they stand before God, that He will not judge them. They think that He will simply overlook their sins. Adolph Hitler was responsible for unspeakable atrocities and the murder of millions of people. Can you imagine God speaking to Adolph Hitler and saying, "You tortured and murdered millions of people but since I am good and loving, it's not a problem. You can go to Heaven." No, because God is absolutely good, He is a God of absolute justice. He will repay every single sin. The question is, are people going to pay the penalty for their own sins (being eternally separated from God in a place of torment) or are they going to put their faith in Jesus Christ who suffered the punishment that you and I deserve.

At the cross, we see the ultimate sacrifice; God the Father, the Perfect, Holy, Righteous, Almighty God, gave His only Son to suffer and die for us. God poured out the wrath that you and I deserve, on His beloved Son. Jesus, God the Son, Perfect, Holy, Righteous and Sinless, willingly came to give His life as a perfect sacrifice to pay the penalty for your sins and mine.

If you don't really believe that God loves you, and loves you a lot, then you might want to put this book down (maybe even for two or three days) and pray about it. Ask God to help you to know how deep His love is for you, and ask Him to help you understand more about the sacrifice that Jesus (God in human flesh) made for you on the cross.

If you breeze past this point and don't realize that God loves you personally, you may find yourself years from now still wondering why you feel like you can never be good enough for God. It's a very hard life trying to be good enough for God. In fact, it's impossible. We will never live a day in our life when we are perfect. Should we be discouraged by that fact and throw our hands up and say, "Then why try?" No, instead we should cry out to our merciful and loving Savior and say, "Thank You Jesus, for dying for my sins. I want to live for You because You love me so incredibly much."

> If you breeze past this point and don't realize that God loves you personally, you may find yourself years from now still wondering why you feel like you can never be good enough for God.

> Life is not about trying to live a perfect life in order to be good enough for God. Life is about responding to God's love.

Life is not about trying to live a perfect life in order to be good enough for God. Life is about responding to God's love. The Apostle Paul said, "The love of Christ compels us."[11] It's His love for us that motivates us to want to live for Him. John the Apostle said, "In this is love, not that we loved God, but that He loved us and

---

[11] 2 Corinthians 5:14

sent His Son…for our sins."[12] Life is not about us trying to measure up to God's standards, it's about responding to His tremendous love for us, that He demonstrated by Jesus coming to this earth and dying on the cross. As the Apostle Paul said "…God demonstrates His own love toward us, in that while we were still sinners, Christ died for us."[13]

It's been said that we as Christians work "from the cross, not to the cross." In other words, we shouldn't try to work hard enough to deserve a relationship with God. We could never work hard enough or be good enough. Our relationship with God is a free gift. As the Apostle Paul said, "For by grace you have been saved through faith; and that not of yourselves, it is the gift of God; not as a result of works, so that no one may boast."[14] So we don't work "to the cross," trying to establish our righteousness before God. We work "from the cross," realizing that He has already declared us righteous because of our faith in Jesus Christ and our life should be lived out as a response to His love for us. If we want to live lives of knowing God's will, we need to know that God loves us. Secondly, in order to live lives of knowing God's will, we need to know that God's will for us is good.

His plans for you are good

This is important for us to realize. God wants the best for us. We can totally trust Him. He is perfect in

---

[12] 1 John 4:10

[13] Romans 5:8

[14] Ephesians 2:8-9 (NASB)

wisdom, He is all-knowing, and He is love. The God we worship and serve is the God who says, "For I know the thoughts that I think toward you, says the LORD, thoughts of peace and not of evil, to give you a future and a hope."[15] Another translation of that verse reads "'For I know the plans that I have for you,' declares the LORD, 'plans for welfare and not for calamity, to give you a future and a hope.'"[16] Don't you like the sound of that? Peace, not evil; welfare, not calamity; a future and a hope?

God knows you better than you know yourself. He knows your thoughts, your feelings, your desires and dreams, your fears, your past, your present, your future, your natural talents and abilities, your spiritual gifts, your strengths and weaknesses, your physical condition and your health. He knows what you are facing right now, and what you will face. If anyone can come up with a great plan for your life, it's God.

> When we are in Heaven, not a single one of us will look back at anything that God planned for us, and say, "Well, that might not have been the best plan, but it worked." or "I could have thought of a better way of doing that."

When we are in Heaven, not a single one of us will look back at anything that God planned for us, and say, "Well, that might not have been the best plan, but it worked," or "I could have thought of a better way of

---

[15] Jeremiah 29:11
[16] Jeremiah 29:11 (NASB)

doing that." No, we will all have the same thing to say about God's plans- "Perfect." God's ways are perfect,[17] His thoughts are perfect and His will for you is perfect.[18] As King David said, "Blessed is that man who makes the LORD his trust..."[19] and "Many, O LORD my God, are Your wonderful works which You have done; And Your thoughts toward us cannot be recounted to You in order; If I would declare and speak of them, They are more than can be numbered."[20]

God's will for us is good. That's so simple and basic but we need to reflect on that over and over so that when we don't understand why the Lord is leading us in a certain direction, or when hard times come along and we don't understand why, we will not become embittered against God. When trials come, we want to be able to go through them like Job, who, although he went through tremendous hardships, said "Though He slay me, yet will I trust Him."[21]

As we grow closer to the Lord and see how good His plans are, we, like King David, will learn to say, "It is God who arms me with strength, and makes my way perfect."[22] It's no wonder the Psalmist wrote, "It is good to give thanks to the LORD, and to sing praises to Your name, O Most High; to declare Your

---

[17] Psalm 18:30, 2 Samuel 22:31
[18] Romans 12:2
[19] Psalm 40:4
[20] Psalm 40:5
[21] Job 13:15
[22] Psalm 18:32

lovingkindness in the morning, and Your faithfulness every night."[23]

Don't blame it on God

Some people think that since God is sovereign over the universe, that whatever happens is by God's design and that He wants it to happen. If that were true, then we could say that God is responsible for everything that happens. Acts of terrorism, murder, theft etc. could all be blamed on God. As we have already seen in the Bible, this is totally contrary to God's character. God is good and everything about Him is good. Scripture tells us "His kingdom rules over all,"[24] but that is very different from saying "His kingdom causes all." At times God will bring calamity and judgment but it is always for perfectly good reasons. God's ways are perfect.

God is omnipotent (all powerful). Many of the things that happen in the world are caused by Him. He rules over the entire universe.[25] On the other hand, many of the things that happen are not caused by Him, they are just allowed by Him. There are many examples of this mentioned in the Bible. In the book of Jeremiah we are told of a time when the people of Jerusalem had committed sins that were so horrible, that God said He had not commanded them to be done, and that they had never even entered into His mind.[26] The Apostle Paul

---

[23] Psalm 92:1-2
[24] Psalm 103:19
[25] Psalm 103:19
[26] Jeremiah 19:5

tells us about unbelievers, saying "And even as they did not like to retain God in their knowledge, God gave them over to a debased mind, to do those things which are not fitting."[27] God doesn't cause people to sin but He does allow us to sin.

God could have made people to be like robots. He could have programmed us to choose to do the right thing in every situation. Then we would not have the ability to choose to sin. The world would be perfect. Or would it? Would a loving parent want to control every movement of their children, not allowing them to choose any of their own actions?

> Would a loving parent want to control every movement of their children, not allowing them to choose any of their own actions?

In God's infinite wisdom and love, He has chosen to create mankind with the ability to make choices. His desire is that we would each choose to have a loving relationship with Him, and He has given us the ability to love. Without the ability to choose, there would be no love.

Let's say for example that we were technologically advanced enough to create a robot to be a perfect husband. When the robot came home from a long day's work, the robot could say to its wife, "It's great to be home. You are beautiful. I love you. I will take out the trash now." While those words might sound like music to some women, you have to admit that there would be

---

[27] Romans 1:28

something missing. If the statement "I love you" was just part of the robot's programming, it would not really be love. In order to love, you must have the ability to choose. Of course, the fact that people are created with the ability to choose, means people can choose not to love God, and to love evil.

In the book of Genesis, we are told the story of Joseph, who was betrayed by his ten brothers. They sold him into slavery and then deceived their father Jacob, leading him to believe that Joseph, his most beloved son, had been killed by wild animals. The result was that Jacob was heartbroken. Losing his son was almost too much for him to bear. He spent more than 22 years thinking that Joseph, his beloved son, was dead. Joseph's brothers spent those years with guilty consciences, knowing that they had deceived their father, causing him tremendous grief, and knowing that they had sinned horribly against their brother. In addition to that, Joseph lived for many years as a slave and then was wrongfully imprisoned for over two years.

Through a series of events, God eventually promoted Joseph to a position of second in charge of the entire nation of Egypt. Joseph was able to deliver the Israelites from a famine and make a way for them to travel to Egypt where they would grow from few in number into a great nation. Joseph forgave his brothers and said to them, "But as for you, you meant evil against me; but God meant it for good."[28]

---

[28] Genesis 50:20

God's perfect will, God's permissive will

It could be said that God has a "perfect will" (that which pleases God) and a "permissive will" (that which He is willing to allow even though it involves sin). Joseph's brothers committed terrible sins against Joseph and their father, and yet God worked it out so that many people's lives were saved. God was not responsible for the sins of Joseph's brothers, but he "meant it for good." In His permissive will, He allowed bad things to happen and then He caused things to work together to end up with very good results. He is on the throne of the universe and "works all things according to the counsel of His will."[29] In spite of the sinful choices that people make, God's purposes will still be accomplished.

Some might ask, "Well, if God is going to work it all out anyway, why not do whatever I want?" As we can see from the lives of Joseph and his brothers, many years of pain and suffering resulted from their sinful choices. It is always better to choose to follow God's perfect will.

> In spite of the sinful choices people make, God's purposes will still be accomplished.

Once we become Christians, God doesn't take away our ability to choose. Some people mistakenly think that as Christians, doing God's will just happens on its own. "It's all good," they say. If that were true, we wouldn't need to try to do God's will because it would happen

---

[29] Ephesians 1:11

"automatically." Like robots, everything we do would be just what our Creator designed us to do. That's not how it works. Whether people are Christians or not, God gives us the ability to make choices.

It is wonderful that as Christians, God's Holy Spirit is working in our lives. In the book of Philippians, the Apostle Paul says to obey the Lord, "for it is God who works in you both to will and to do for His good pleasure."[30] That's a wonderful truth.

God guides us and leads us into things He wants us to do, but we must choose to follow His leading. As Joshua said, "…choose for yourselves this day whom you will serve… But as for me and my house, we will serve the LORD."[31]

> As Joshua said, "…choose for yourselves this day whom you will serve… But as for me and my house, we will serve the LORD."
> - Joshua 24:15

Every one of us is unique. There are things that God has designed just for you to do. As Paul says, "For we are His workmanship, created in Christ Jesus for good works, which God prepared beforehand that we should walk in them."[32] God loves you. He wants to use you and He has wonderful plans for your life- Say "Yes" to Him.

In the following chapters of this book, we will be exploring ways of knowing God's will that can bring us

---

[30] Philippians 2:13
[31] Joshua 24:15
[32] Ephesians 2:10

closer to Him than we have ever been, and help us develop a sensitivity to His leading that we have never known. Truly, He wants to guide us "with His eye."

Heavenly Father, Thank you for loving me so much that You sent Your Son to suffer and die for me. Help me to know on a deeper level, how much You love me. I know that I deserve Your judgment. Thank You for showing me mercy instead. Please help me to see how good Your plans for me are. Please help me to trust You completely. I love you. In Jesus' name I pray, Amen.

There are five key areas that we will be looking at in this book as we look at how we can know the will of God. They can be memorized easily by linking them together in the acronym- C.R.O.S.S. In the next chapter, we will look at what may be the most important thing of all in terms of knowing God's will- the "C" in the C.R.O.S.S.

3

C. - Commit

"I beseech you therefore, brethren, by the mercies of God, that you present your bodies a living sacrifice, holy, acceptable to God, which is your reasonable service. And do not be conformed to this world, but be transformed by the renewing of your mind, that you may prove what is that good and acceptable and perfect will of God."

-Romans 12:1-2

Johnny

As soon as Johnny walked into the kitchen after getting home from school, he was greeted by the wonderful smell of cookies baking in the oven. "Can I have some cookies?" he excitedly asked his mother. "Of course," his mother said. "There are a few things I'd like to ask you to do before you have any cookies, however. First, would you please rake up the leaves in the backyard?" "Sure." replied Johnny happily. He walked out the door of the kitchen into the backyard and walked back in the door three seconds later. "Now what would you like me to do?" he asked. "Hmm," his mother replied, "Did you rake up the leaves in the backyard?" "Nope, I didn't want to rake the leaves, but now what would you like me to do?" he asked. "I want you to rake up the leaves in the backyard," his mother replied.

Like Johnny with his mother, we can ignore God's leading because it doesn't sound good to us, and then want God to guide us into the next thing, thinking that we might like it better.

> **We can ignore God's leading because it doesn't sound good to us, and then want God to guide us into the next thing, thinking that we might like it better.**

The first two verses in Romans Chapter 12 have some tremendous insights into knowing the will of God. One of them is so simple that we can almost miss it as we read those two verses- A key to knowing God's will is being willing to do God's will. This brings us to the first letter in the C.R.O.S.S.- C. for Commit.

The Apostle Paul tells us that we should present our bodies as a living sacrifice to God. That's not how the sentence starts, however. It begins with, "I beseech you therefore, brethren, by the mercies of God" or as another translation renders it, "Therefore I urge you, brethren, by the mercies of God"[1]

> **A key to knowing God's will is being willing to do God's will.**

In the first 11 chapters of the book of Romans, the Apostle Paul explains a lot about the mercy of God. He turns a corner here and says in effect, "Therefore, seeing

---

[1] Romans 12:1 (NASB)

how merciful God is, present yourselves as a living sacrifice to Him." What we believe about God determines how we behave toward God, and as we've looked at in the previous chapter, our motivation for doing God's will comes as we think about His great love and mercy toward us. God is worthy of being surrendered to.

When Paul says that we should "present" ourselves to God, he is talking about a "once and for all" commitment. It's kind of like jumping out of a plane with a parachute on. When people go skydiving, they don't cruise along in the plane with one foot hanging out the door. Well, they might do that, but it's not skydiving. Once they are outside of the plane, hurling towards earth at a high speed, then they are skydiving. Paul is telling us that we should make a 100%, totally surrendered commitment to God.

The verse tells us that we should be "holy," which means

> **It is completely reasonable to commit ourselves 100% to God.**

we should be "separated" or set apart from sin and set apart for God, and that we should be "acceptable" (which in the original language, could be translated as "well pleasing") to God. We shouldn't be cruising along in our Christian life with one foot hanging out the door of the plane.

Paul says that it's our "reasonable service." It is completely reasonable to commit ourselves 100% to God. There is a hymn entitled "I surrender all." The hymn was written in 1896 and has been sung by millions of people over the years. The refrain to the hymn is as follows-

"I surrender all,

I surrender all,

all to thee, my blessed Savior,

I surrender all."

Our natural tendency is to want to sing that song a little differently. We want to sing something along the lines of-

"I surrender some,

I surrender some,

some to thee, my blessed Savior,

I surrender some."

If you really think about it however, it's easy to see that giving ourselves as a living sacrifice is perfectly reasonable. God created the universe. He is all powerful, all knowing, and He is perfect in wisdom and love. In His mercy, He made the ultimate sacrifice for us and His plans for us are good. It would be crazy not to completely surrender to Him.

Jesus is Lord

In the New Testament, Jesus is called "Savior" 16 times. He is called "Lord" 747 times. He is our Savior but it is noteworthy that He is referred to as Lord almost 750 times. In the book of Philippians we are told that "… at the name of Jesus every knee will bow, of those who are in heaven and on earth and under the earth, and that every tongue will confess that Jesus Christ is Lord."[2] The word "Lord" could be translated as "Master." Jesus is the One with authority over the entire universe. As the Apostle Peter said, "He is Lord of all."[3]

> In the New Testament, Jesus is called "Savior" 16 times. He is called "Lord" 747 times.

Some people think of themselves as Christians but do not confess Jesus as Lord in their lives. They may feel more comfortable thinking of Him as "the Man upstairs" or just their "buddy." Other people think of Jesus as their "fire insurance" and might go so far as to admit that He is the "Son of God," but Jesus is Lord. He is God.[4] He created the entire universe[5] and we will all stand before Him on judgment day.[6] Those who reject the authority of God take the same path as Lucifer, who said "I will… I will… I will…"[7] and they will share his same eternal destiny.[8]

As the Bible tells us plainly, "…if you confess with your mouth the Lord Jesus and believe in your heart that God has raised Him from the dead, you will be

[2] Philippians 2:10-11 (NASB)
[3] Acts 10:36
[4] John 1:1, Hebrews 1:8
[5] John 1:3, Colossians 1:16-17
[6] John 5:22
[7] Isaiah 14:12-13
[8] Revelation 20:10,15; Matthew 25:41

saved."[9] And "whoever calls on the name of the LORD shall be saved."[10]

God gives us the choice whether or not to surrender to His authority. We can choose to say, "Nobody's going to tell me what to do. I am the captain of my ship," or we can choose to acknowledge God as God-by surrendering to the One who loved us so much that He died for us. As the Apostle Paul said, "He died that we might no longer live for ourselves but for Him who died and rose again on our behalf."[11]

Acknowledging God

The book of Proverbs says, "In all your ways, acknowledge Him and He shall direct your paths."[12] Acknowledging God is a matter of allowing God into your life. It is saying, "Ok, Lord. What should I do now?" Notice that we should acknowledge God "in all our ways."[13]

Our natural tendency is to want Him to guide us in some things and to only turn some areas of our lives over to His control, but we should turn everything over to Him, not only by making a one-time decision of surrender, but throughout every day, as situations arise. We need to learn to continually look to Him for guidance. We will explore how to do that in this book.

---

[9] Romans 10:9
[10] Romans 10:13
[11] 2Corinthians 5:15
[12] Proverbs 3:6
[13] Proverbs 3:6

Don't put your hand on the stove

We can be like a child who is warned by their parent, "Don't put your hand on the stove. It's hot." In many cases, what is the child's next word? "Ouch!"

Some people think that if they don't follow God's will, their life will be better. We all know people who seem determined to learn things the hard way. The Bible is filled with examples of people going through very hard times, simply because they are not willing to obey God and do His will.

The children of Israel had walked from Egypt to the border of the "promised land," a land "flowing with milk and honey."[14] Just a few more steps and they would have been there, in a land tremendously rich in natural resources; a land of abundance that was filled with the blessings of God. Rather than choosing to believe God however, most of the children of Israel chose not to obey Him. As a result, they spent the next 40 years wandering around in the wilderness until the last one of them that had chosen the path of disobedience, died.

> The Bible is filled with examples of people going through very hard times, simply because they are not willing to obey God and do His will.

We can learn from their experiences and take heed to the warning of the Bible- "Therefore, as the Holy

---

[14] Deuteronomy 6:3

Spirit says: 'Today, if you will hear His voice, do not harden your hearts as in the rebellion, in the day of trial in the wilderness.'"[15]

Most children have probably heard their parents say something like, "You can do this the easy way or you can do it the hard way." Does a parent tell their child not to put their hand on a hot stove top because the parent is mean and wants to deprive their child of good things? No, they warn them because they know more than the child does, and they love their child. God loves us and He wants to bless us by guiding us into His perfect will.

If we want to experience that "good and acceptable and perfect will of God,"[16] commitment to God is the starting point. Will we fall short of perfect obedience? Definitely, as the Apostle John tells us, "If we say that we have no sin, we deceive ourselves, and the truth is not in us."[17] But our aim should be to walk in obedience to the Lord.

> **If we want to experience that "good and acceptable and perfect will of God," commitment to God is the starting point.**

As we continue to walk in obedience to God's leading, we can enjoy intimacy with God. In the process, we will not only develop more of a sensitivity to His leading, we will grow in maturity as well. We can do this the easy way, or we can do it the hard way.

---

[15] Hebrews 3:7-8
[16] Romans 12:2
[17] 1 John 1:8

Jesus, the ultimate example

As Christians, we are all called to be "disciples" of Christ. The word "disciple" means "learner" or "follower." Jesus had quite a bit to say about doing the will of God. He said, "...I have come down from heaven, not to do My own will, but the will of Him who sent Me."[18] It's what He came for. He left Heaven and came to the earth for the purpose of doing God's will. He told His disciples, "My food is to do the will of Him who sent Me, and to finish His work..."[19] That's like saying, "I live on doing God's will." Jesus was 100% totally committed to doing the will of God.

On the night that Jesus was betrayed by Judas, He was praying in the Garden of Gethsemane. He knew that He would be crucified the next day. Even though Jesus had never committed a single sin, He knew that the sins of the whole world[20] were going to be laid on Him. He would suffer an incredibly painful and slow death and experience a separation from His Father. Jesus prayed to God saying, "Father, if it is Your will, take this cup away from Me; nevertheless not My will, but Yours, be done."[21]

Jesus was consumed

> Jesus was consumed with a passion to do the will of God and He was willing to pay any price. Nothing mattered more to Him than pleasing His Father and doing His will.

---

[18] John 6:38
[19] John 4:34
[20] 1 John 2:2
[21] Luke 22:42

with a passion to do the will of God and He was willing to pay any price. Nothing mattered more to Him than pleasing His Father and doing His will.

Jesus went to the ultimate extreme to do God's will. Some good news for us is that God will not ask us to do the same thing that Jesus did. You and I will not have the sins of the world placed on our shoulders. What Jesus went through for us will always be far more than what God will ever ask from us.

You can also know that when we get to Heaven, we will not look back at our lives and say, "Wow. God sure asked a lot from me." No, when we get to Heaven, we will say, "Truly, God's will for me was perfect and He is worthy of a million times more than what I did for Him." Jesus paid the ultimate price for us.

> When we get to Heaven, we will say, "Truly, God's will for me was perfect and He is worthy of a million times more than what I did for Him."

Jesus is also the ultimate example. If you are seeking to do the will of God, you are truly seeking a good thing. You are following in the footsteps of Jesus, who said "I do not seek My own will but the will of the Father who sent Me."[22]

> If you are seeking to do the will of God, you are truly seeking a good thing. You are following in the footsteps of Jesus.

---

[22] John 5:30

Why get married, move, change jobs or make any other big decision

A pastor was speaking to a class of about 40 young adult students at a school of evangelism. "There is only one reason to get married." he said. "What is that reason? Before you answer, let me tell you what it's not. It's not because you love each other." The students sat in kind of a stunned silence. After what seemed like several minutes had passed, a girl finally raised her hand. The pastor looked at her. "Sex?" she said, half jokingly. "Nope." replied the pastor. After more silence, the pastor answered his own question, "The only reason to get married is because God tells you to get married."

It doesn't matter how big the decision is, or how strongly we may feel about something. We will always be making the right decision if Jesus is the Lord of our decision making process. We are told to bring "every thought into captivity to the obedience of Christ."[23] He knows everything and if we know that He is guiding us in our decisions, we will never have to wonder, "Did I marry the right person?" or "Did I take the right job?" or "Was I supposed to move to this city?" or "Did God really call me to China?" We can have a tremendous amount of peace in our lives even in the midst of the storms of life, if we are surrendering to Jesus as our Lord.

As we will be exploring in this book, in order for Jesus to be the Lord of our life, we need to listen when

---

[23] 2 Corinthians 10:5

God speaks to us. Listening is a missing ingredient in many people's relationship with God. This brings us to a vital component in our relationship with God. It is also essential to a life of knowing God's will.

Devoted to prayer

Prayer is awesome! Many Christians have no idea how powerful,[24] fulfilling, refreshing, comforting, healing, life changing, and world changing, prayer can be. We can go through our whole lives without ever realizing that through prayer, we have the privilege of being able to accomplish things that many of us believe are impossible. If people only knew. Prayer can radically change our lives, give us an intimacy with God that we didn't know was possible, and can fast track us to knowing God's will in ways that nothing else can.

> Prayer can radically change our life, give us an intimacy with God that we didn't know was possible, and can fast track us to knowing God's will in ways that nothing else can.

Our God is the One who said, "Call to Me, and I will answer you, and show you great and mighty things, which you do not know."[25] It's no wonder that the Apostle Paul tells us that we should be "continuing steadfastly in prayer"[26] or as another translation reads, we should be "devoted to prayer."[27]

---

[24] The power is of course, not in the prayers, but in God who hears and answers our prayers.

[25] Jeremiah 33:3

[26] Romans 12:12

Think about how important communication is in a relationship. It's vital. In fact, that's what a relationship is- a connection, an association, an involvement. This explanation of what a relationship is may sound simple and basic, but as Christians, we can miss it when it comes to God. Just as two people must communicate with each other in order to have a close relationship, we must pray.

When many people think of prayer, they think of drudgery- work that we are obligated to do, like having to mow the lawn or wash dishes. They're missing it. While prayer does involve effort, if you ask anyone who knows the Lord and has experienced the blessings of a life of "continuing steadfastly in prayer," they will tell you that it's so much more than just work.

Ask a newlywed if they enjoy being with their spouse (at least most newlyweds). Ask a happily married couple who have been together for 45 years if they enjoy being together. They will not say that they think of being together as work or drudgery.

> **A boring prayer life is an undeveloped prayer life.**

While spending time with a person you love deeply can be a wonderful experience, it doesn't compare to the potential of spending time with the Creator of the universe who loves you with an everlasting love. God wants to spend time with you. He loves you.

---

[27] Romans 12:12 (NASB)

Prayer is boring and monotonous to a lot of people but that's because they have only scratched the surface of what prayer can be. A boring prayer life is an undeveloped prayer life. Prayer can be developed into a

> Prayer can be developed into a communion with God that can be the most wonderful and satisfying thing in your life.

communion with God that can be the most wonderful and satisfying thing in your life. It can give you peace and joy throughout your day, a peace and joy that can't be found anywhere else but in His presence. As the Scriptures tell us, "In Your presence is fullness of joy."[28]

There are many blessings that come through having a life that is devoted to prayer that we are not going to look at now (that's a subject for another book) but let's take a look at some of the blessings in regard to knowing God's will.

The Apostle James said, "If any of you lacks wisdom, let him ask of God..."[29] We can have wisdom given to us by the Creator and Sustainer of the universe, the One who is perfectly wise and

> God invented water, color, light, the atom, the rainbow, the soft breeze and the sunset before any of them had ever existed.

all-knowing. God invented water, color, light, the atom, the rainbow, the soft breeze and the sunset before any of them had ever existed. That's amazing.

---

[28] Psalm 16:11
[29] James 1:5

Have you ever thought about sunrises and sunsets? Not only are they beautiful, but twenty four hours a day, there is a ring of sunrise and sunset going on around the globe. At every moment, there is a circle of beauty in the sky, 25,000 miles around, being made by the sunrise and sunset occurring on earth.

That's just one aspect of the beautiful creation that God has made and He is the God who wants to guide us and have us spend time alone with Him every day.

James said, "...you do not have because you do not ask."[30] Much of the time, we don't know the will of God because we don't ask about it. Jesus said "Ask, and it will be given to you; seek, and you will find; knock, and it will be opened to you."[31] The words "Ask," "seek," and "knock" are in the "present tense" in the original language and imply a continuing action. The passage could also be translated as "Keep on asking, keep on seeking, and keep on knocking."

The Apostle James also tells us that when we ask for wisdom from God, we should "ask in faith, with no doubting."[32] Like someone who is floating in the ocean, holding on to a lifeline thrown from a rescue ship, we should hold on to the promises of God. Have faith that your prayers for wisdom and guidance will be answered because the One holding the other end of the lifeline is the Captain of our rescue ship- Almighty God.

---

[30] James 4:2
[31] Matthew 7:7; Luke 11:9
[32] James 1:6

While we are told to be "continuing steadfastly in prayer,"[33] it could easily be said that Americans are instead "continuing steadfastly in watching television." According to surveys, American Christians, on average, spend about *5 minutes a day in prayer.* On the other hand, Americans, on average, spend about *5 hours a day watching television* and about an hour a day on the internet.

In the book of Isaiah, God says, "For My house shall be called a house of prayer for all nations."[34] As Christians, our body is a temple of the Holy Spirit.[35] God's Spirit indwells us and His desire is that each of us would be a "house of prayer."

That phrase should define our lives. Why go through life as a "house of watching television," a "house of self-seeking," or a "house of work," when we can live our lives truly walking with, and knowing, the Creator of the universe?

It's been said that "No Christian is greater than their prayer life." This is not being shared to make you feel like a "bad Christian," or to make you feel guilty, but to encourage you to commit to making prayer an important part of your life.

Here are a few thoughts that might help you as you seek to become more of a "house of prayer" and seek to know God's will -

---

33 Romans 12:12
34 Isaiah 56:7
35 1 Corinthians 6:19

➤ Commit to prayer[36]- Can we be committed to God without being committed to prayer? Going to bed earlier and waking up early to your alarm clock won't feel good, but once you have spent some time in prayer, you'll be glad you got out of bed. (You might also want to ask the Lord to wake you up when He wants you to get up to pray, and watch what happens.)

➤ Make appointments with God and keep them[37]- Schedule daily times of prayer. Ask the Lord to put an amount of time on your heart that He might want you to aim for every day in prayer- whether it be ½ hour, an hour, two hours, or whatever the Lord might put on your heart. Don't beat yourself up when you fall short. God doesn't want you to live by a set of rules. He wants to be with you.

➤ Spend time worshipping and praising God[38]- It's good to sing to the Lord.[39] Don't worry about how well you sing. God loves the sound of you singing to Him.

➤ Thank God for lots of things[40]- Big and small things- like God's love, salvation, eternal life, the Holy Spirit, the Bible, fellowship... and things like your eyes, your lungs... the sun, rain...

---

[36] Romans 12:12
[37] 1 Timothy 4:7
[38] John 4:24; Psalm 22:26
[39] Psalm 47:6; 147:1
[40] Philippians 4:6

➢ Commit to the Lord in prayer[41]- As you seek to find out the will of God in your times of prayer, continually surrender afresh to the Lord.

➢ Confess your sins to God[42]- (Ask Him to bring them to your mind and wait silently before the Lord. Quite often, He'll remind you of some.)

➢ Spend time waiting on the Lord[43]- Try to be sensitive to the Lord's leading as you spend time in prayer. Don't just talk to God, spend time listening.[44] What God has to say to us is more important than what we have to say to God. (We'll explore this later in the book.)

> **What God has to say to us is more important than what we have to say to God.**

➢ Spend time asking[45]- For yourself and for others (intercession). A prayer list is helpful for this part of your prayer time. A world map is also a great aid, as well as a book like *Operation World,* by Jason Mandryk. Try to allow the Lord to lead your prayer times.[46] Ask Him what and who He wants you to pray about (and then give Him time to put things on your heart to pray). We can accomplish more through prayer than we can

---

[41] Mark 12:30
[42] 1 John 1:9
[43] Isaiah 40:31
[44] Matthew 17:5
[45] Philippians 4:6
[46] Ephesians 6:18

through anything else in our lives- "Unless the LORD builds the house, they labor in vain who build it.[47]

➤ "Pray without ceasing"[48]- Try to develop a habit of praying throughout the day. As you practice at it, you will find yourself communing with the Lord more often and longer during the day.

Prayer is in essence, communion with God. It's about opening our hearts to God, surrendering our lives to Him and seeking God, Himself. It's not only about seeking what He can give us. After all, God is the greatest blessing we could ever receive.

> **Prayer is in essence, communion with God. It's about opening our hearts to God, surrendering our lives to Him and seeking God Himself.**

He will give you the desires of your heart

Psalm 37:4 says, "Delight yourself in the LORD; and He will give you the desires of your heart."[49] That verse is a conditional promise- *If* you delight in the Lord, *then* He will give you the desires of your heart. A key to knowing the will of God is living a life of praise, worship and thanksgiving- delighting in Him. As we delight in Him, He will be putting desires in our hearts and He will satisfy those desires as well. What a wonderful truth- As we delight in Him, we will want

---

[47] Psalm 127:1
[48] 1 Thessalonians 5:17
[49] Psalm 37:4 (NASB)

what God wants (that which is best for us and others), and then He will give us what we want.

This truth ties in so well with the verse we looked at in the beginning of the chapter; In view of God's mercy, as we present our bodies a living sacrifice and have our minds renewed (and delight in the Lord), we will "prove what the will of God is" (and have the desires of our heart).

We want to "walk in the spirit,"[50] and to "walk with God."[51] In order to do that, we must stay close to the Lord. James tells us, "Draw near to God and He will draw near to you."[52] It's a matter of the heart. Knowing God's will is a byproduct of our love for, and our intimacy with, the Lord.

As we commit ourselves to the Lord and seek to present ourselves as a living sacrifice, we will be far more open to hearing from the Lord and knowing His will. God gives His Holy Spirit to those who obey

> It's a matter of the heart. Knowing God's will is a byproduct of our love for, and our intimacy with, the Lord.

Him,[53] and as we love and choose to obey Him, we will see God working out His "good and acceptable and perfect will" in and through our lives.

---

[50] Galatians 5:16
[51] Genesis 6:9
[52] James 4:8
[53] Acts 5:32

Heavenly Father, You are so wonderful and merciful and You are worthy of all honor, glory and praise. Thank you for giving Your Son for me. I surrender to You. Jesus, You are Lord. I choose to allow You to truly be the Lord of my life. Help me to commit my life to You and help me to be a person of prayer. I love you, Amen.

As we will see in the next chapter, God definitely wants to speak to us and it's wonderful to be able to hear Him when He does.

4

R. - Read

"Your word is a lamp to my feet and a light to my path."

-Psalm 119:105

My wife and I were travelling in a city that is a few hundred miles away from our home. At one point as we drove along, discussing which way to go, my wife said something to me about being lost. I replied, "I'm not lost. I just don't know where I am." People don't like being lost and we don't like admitting it when we are lost. We want to know that we are going in the right direction.

> The difference between hearing from God and not hearing from Him is the difference between a dry, tedious life and an abundant life.

Walking in the light of God's Word

The value of hearing God when He speaks to us cannot be overstated. The difference between hearing from God and not hearing from Him is the difference between a dry, tedious life and an abundant life- a life of peace and joy, a life of knowing that God is guiding you.

Jesus said, "The words that I speak to you are spirit and they are life."[1]

None of us want to guess what God's will is. We want to know it. Do you ever read or hear something and it just clicks? It rings so true that you wish you'd thought of it yourself. God's guidance can be like that and one of the

If you want to know God's will, read God's Word.

ways that God speaks clearly to us is through the Bible. This brings us to the "R" in C.R.O.S.S.- Read. If you want to know God's will, read God's Word.

When God was guiding the writers of the Old and New Testaments, He knew exactly where we would be right now, and He knew what He would want to say to us. It is amazing that thousands of years after the Bible was written, hundreds of millions of people can read it, and it can speak to each one of us.

The Bible is different from any other book. The words of the Bible are perfect in wisdom and truth, and God wants to speak directly to us through the Bible about our individual situations.

Some people wonder whether the Bible is reliable. It is- absolutely. For example, when it comes to major world events, the Bible is more accurate about today's news than the headline news reports, but it was written over a period of 1500 years, and was completed almost 2,000 years ago. We watch as a global government is

---

[1] John 6:63

being formed[2] and as nations gather together in opposition against Israel.[3] Those are just two of many events that the Bible predicts will happen in "the latter days."[4] In the first 35 verses of the book of Daniel chapter 11, there are 135 specific prophecies that have been fulfilled exactly as written. Jesus fulfilled more than 300 prophecies written about Him, including where He would be born,[5] that He would be betrayed by a friend,[6] and how He would die.[7] The prediction that He would have His hands and feet pierced is an amazing prophecy made about 1,000 years before Jesus was born. Crucifixion (a form of execution which involves piercing a person's hands and feet) wasn't even invented until hundreds of years after the prophecy was made. And most importantly, the Bible predicted that Jesus would rise from the dead.[8] There were more than 500 people who saw Jesus after He had risen from the dead.[9] The Bible is absolutely trustworthy.

In Isaiah 46:9-10, God says, "'Remember the former things of old, for I am God, and there is no other; I am God, and there is none like Me, declaring the end from the beginning, and from ancient times things that are not yet done, saying, 'My counsel shall stand, and I will do all My pleasure.'" In the New Testament, Jesus said,

---

[2] Daniel 7:23; Revelation 13:7
[3] Ezekiel 38; Zechariah 12:1-3
[4] Revelation 13, Ezekiel 38
[5] Micah 5:2
[6] Psalm 41:9
[7] Psalm 22:16
[8] Psalm 16:10-11
[9] 1 Corinthians 15:6

"Now I tell you before it comes, that when it does come to pass, you may believe that I am He."[10] God in effect, says, "This is how you'll know that I've spoken to you; I'll tell you the future in advance." There is no other book like the Bible. The Bible contains around 2,500 prophecies. About 2,000 of them have already been fulfilled exactly as predicted and the other 500 or so, pertain to the future. Not one single prediction of the Bible has been wrong.

The Bible predicts future events with 100% accuracy and the truths contained in the pages of the Bible have radically changed the lives of hundreds of millions of people. God's word is perfect. As Jesus said, "Heaven and earth will pass away, but My words will by no means pass away."[11]

> In the Bible, God in effect says, "This is how you'll know that I've spoken to you; I'll tell you the future in advance."

The Psalmist wrote "Your word is a lamp to my feet and a light to my path."[12] When that Psalm was written, oil lamps would be carried in front of caravans travelling at night. These lamps would give light to the area and would also make it possible to see which way to go. In the same way today, the word of God "is a lamp to our feet," (it gives light and understanding to our current situations) and "a light to our path" (it shows us which way we should go).

---

[10] John 13:19
[11] Luke 21:33
[12] Psalm 119:105

Staying on the path

Jesus was led by the Holy Spirit into the wilderness where He was tempted by the devil. The Bible tells us three different things that the devil said to Him in an attempt to lead Jesus away from doing the will of God. In each of the three temptations, Jesus responded the same way- He quoted the Scriptures, the Word of God, saying, "It is written… It is written… It is written. . ."[13] Jesus used the Word of God as a weapon against the devil.[14] The Scriptures can also be a powerful weapon in our lives to keep us from straying from God's perfect will.

In Psalm 119, the Psalmist wrote, "Your word I have hidden in my heart, that I might not sin against You."[15] The word "sin" in the original language expresses the idea of missing the mark, going wrong or incurring guilt. If we want to stay on the path and know God's will, we should seek to "hide" God's word in our hearts, or as another translation puts it, to "treasure"[16] God's word in our hearts. God's written word is indeed a treasure. A person can spend a lifetime reading and gleaning riches from the Bible and still only

> A person can spend a lifetime reading and gleaning riches from the Bible and still only see a fraction of what the Bible contains. It's a well that never runs dry.

---

[13] Matthew 4:4,6,10
[14] Ephesians 6:17
[15] Psalm 119:11
[16] Psalm 119:11 NASB

see a fraction of what the Bible contains. It is a well that never runs dry.

The Apostle Paul tells us that "All Scripture is given by inspiration of God…"[17] The word "inspiration" in that verse literally means "God-breathed." This is very different than when someone sees a beautiful sunset and is inspired to write a poem about it. God Himself is the One who has given us the Bible. The writers of the Bible were not in a trance, writing down divine dictation, but they were moved by the Holy Spirit, led by God, to write what they wrote. The Bible is exactly what God wants to communicate to us.

Getting blessed

The first Psalm starts out, "Blessed is the man who walks not in the counsel of the ungodly, nor stands in the path of sinners, nor sits in the seat of the scornful; But his delight is in the law of the LORD, and in His law he meditates day and night. He shall be like a tree planted by the rivers of water, that brings forth its fruit in its season, whose leaf also shall not wither; and whatever he does shall prosper."[18]

We all want to be blessed. The word "blessed" in Psalm 1 could also be translated as "happy." We are told that we will be happy and blessed if we delight in the Law (or "instruction, direction") of the Lord, and if we meditate on His instruction "day and night."

---

[17] 2 Timothy 3:16.
[18] Psalm 1:1-3

The first blessing that is promised if we delight in and meditate on (or reflect on, contemplate) God's Word, is that we will be "like a tree planted by the rivers of water." What a picture of nourishment. A tree is constantly watered if it is planted next to a river, but the promise is even richer than that. The promise is that we will be like a tree planted next to "rivers of water." What is more nourishing and sustaining for a tree than being planted next to a river? Being planted between *two* rivers. It is continually nourished and fed.

The second blessing mentioned is that of yielding "fruit in its season." In God's perfect timing, we all want our lives to be fruitful, to live lives that makes a difference- lives of significance.

The third blessing is that of having leaves that don't "wither." We don't want to have aspects of our lives that are dry and withered. We all want to be full of life.

The fourth blessing mentioned is prospering in whatever we do. Wouldn't that be great? To prosper in whatever you do?

These are the blessings promised to us if we will delight in and meditate on the Scriptures (and avoid the things mentioned in the beginning of the Psalm). God wants to bless us. Reading God's word leads us on the path to blessings and is a way to hear clearly from God.

> **Reading God's word leads us on the path to blessings and is a way to hear clearly from God.**

If we want to discern God's will as we read the Bible, the key is not just to go through God's Word. The key is allowing God's Word to go through us. It can be a great help to pray before we read, pray as we read, and pray after we read.[19]

By allowing God's Word to penetrate our hearts, we will see things in the Scriptures that we otherwise wouldn't see. When we read God's Word, we shouldn't be in a rush. Instead, we should read slowly enough to allow our minds and hearts to be impacted by what we are reading. We want our hearts to be like the "good ground"[20] that Jesus talked about so that the seeds of God's Word will produce abundant fruit in and through our lives.

> If we want to discern God's will as we read the Bible, the key is not just to go through God's Word. The key is allowing God's Word to go through us.

Two words in Greek

There are two words[21] that are used most often in the original language of the New Testament that are translated as "word" in our English language Bibles. Why would you want to know that? Well, by looking at these two Greek words, we can gain significant insight

---

[19] 1 Thessalonians 5:17

[20] Matthew 13:23; Mark 4:20

[21] There are a couple of other words translated as "word" that are used once or twice but the vast majority of the occurrences of "word" in the New Testament are translated from Logos or Rhema.

into how God speaks to us through the Scriptures. One of the Greek words is "Logos." The other is "Rhema."

Logos

The word "logos" is used more often (330 times) than "rhema" (70 times) in the Bible. Logos could be defined as "word, the expression of thought, reasoning, discourse, speech, instruction." Logos is the word that we get our English word "logic" from. In John Chapter 1, Jesus is called "the Word" (Logos). He is the expression of God's very being. God speaks to us through His Son.[22]

God also speaks to us through the Bible.[23] In the book of Hebrews we are told, "For the word of God is living and powerful..."[24] God's written Word has the

> **The Bible is not just a book about God- It is a book from God.**

power to change our lives. The Bible is not just a book *about* God- it is a book *from* God. As we read God's Word, we see His wisdom and truth. In our quest to know the will of God, the importance of reading God's Word cannot be overstated.

The Bible is filled with wisdom from God and as King Solomon said, "Happy is the man who finds wisdom, and the man who gains understanding; for her proceeds are better than the profits of silver, and her gain than fine gold. She is more precious than rubies,

---

[22] Hebrews 1:2
[23] 2 Timothy 3:16
[24] Hebrews 4:12

and all the things you may desire cannot compare with her."[25]

A few examples

Here are some questions we can ask in order to help determine God's will in a situation, using the Word (logos) of God-

1- Will it bring glory to God?

> "...whatever you do, do all to the glory of God."
> -Romans 10:31

2- Have you prayed about it?

> "If any of you lacks wisdom, let him ask of God..."   -James 1:5

3- What does the Bible say about it?

> "All Scripture is given by inspiration of God, and is profitable for doctrine, for reproof, for correction, for instruction in righteousness."
> -2 Timothy 3:16

4- Does it have the appearance of evil?

> "Abstain from all appearance of evil."
> -1 Thessalonians 5:22 (KJV)

5- What effect does it have on others?

---

[25] Proverbs 3:13-15

"You shall love your neighbor as yourself."
-Romans 14:19

"Therefore let us pursue the things which make for peace and the things by which one may edify another."   -Matthew 22:39

6- Do you have a clear conscience about it?

"I thank God, whom I serve with a pure conscience,"   -2 Timothy 1:3

7- Does it lead to pride or humility?

"...God resists the proud, but gives grace to the humble."   -1 Peter 5:5

8- Does it have the potential to control you?

"All things are lawful for me, but all things are not helpful. All things are lawful for me, but I will not be brought under the power of any."
-1 Corinthians 6:12

Rhema

The other word in Greek that is translated as "word" in the New Testament is "rhema." Rhema is similar in meaning to logos but its meaning is more specifically, "a spoken word" or "an utterance." There are times when God speaks directly to us- when the words of Scripture seem to come alive.

I grew up having no interest in Christianity whatsoever. In fact, Christianity was the one religion that I thought was definitely wrong. After a series of amazing events in my life, I bought a Bible and started reading it. I began in the Gospel of John. As I was reading one day, I read the words of Jesus where He said "You did not choose Me, but I chose you..."[26] It was a "rhema" word from God. The words seemed to jump off the page. I actually spoke my response out loud. I said, "Yeah, that's for sure because I sure didn't choose you!" I suddenly realized that the events that led me to being open to reading the Bible had been orchestrated by God. I was amazed- Jesus had chosen me! That passage of Scripture changed my life. It spoke powerfully to my heart and mind.

Even though there had been a series of what I consider to be miraculous events that led up to the point of my being willing to read the Bible, I didn't receive Jesus until God had spoken to me through His Word. As Scripture says, "Faith comes by hearing, and hearing by the word (rhema) of God."[27]

It wasn't just the wisdom and truth (logos) of the Scriptures that brought me to the point of receiving Jesus as my Lord and Savior, it was a specific passage of Scripture that God used to pierce my heart. Faith is a gift[28] and it comes through God speaking directly to us. As Jesus said, "The words (rhema) that I speak to you are spirit, and they are life."[29]

---

[26] John 15:16
[27] Romans 10:17
[28] Ephesians 2:8-9
[29] John 6:63

It's not only the beginning of our saving relationship with Jesus that comes through hearing the "rhema" word of God. Jesus also said, "Man shall not live by bread alone, but by every word (rhema) that proceeds from the mouth of God."[30] As Christians, we don't just live on food, we live on what God says directly to us. We need to hear from God. It's noteworthy that Jesus compared food, which we eat several times a day, to our need to hear from God. We are nourished physically by food and spiritually by the Word of God. His Words to us are what nourish and sustain us.

> **We are nourished physically by food and spiritually by the Word of God. His words to us are what nourish and sustain us.**

A few examples

The Lord spoke to me through John 15:16 where He said "You did not choose Me, but I chose you…"[31] I believe that He spoke to me again years later through that same passage of Scripture. After saying "I chose you," the verse goes on to say, "…that you should go and bear fruit, and that your fruit should remain…" As I was reading that verse one morning (after being a Christian for about 10 years), it hit me afresh. I had read and heard that verse numerous times but this time it seemed to come alive. Jesus not only chose me, but He chose me that I should bear fruit. Jesus said, "By this

---

[30] Matthew 4:4
[31] John 15:16

My Father is glorified, that you bear much fruit."[32] I didn't see "much fruit," or fruit that would "remain," coming from my life. As I read that verse, I was hit with the reality that God wanted my life to bear a lot of spiritual fruit.

I started to pray about it, "Lord, I want to bear 'much fruit,' fruit that will last for eternity. I want to bring as many people to Heaven with my life as I can." As I continued to pray about it over the next couple of weeks, I believe the Lord spoke to me about it again through the Scriptures. One morning, right after praying about it, I read Acts Chapter 7, verse 3, where it recounts how the Lord called Abraham, "Get out of your country and from your relatives, and come to a land that I will show you." It was another "rhema" word from the Lord. While that verse is truth from God (logos), it was also a specific message (rhema) to me on that morning.

As I read that verse, I was flooded with the thought that God was leading my wife and I to leave Hawaii (where we were born and raised) and move to Texas to serve in the U.S. office of Gospel for Asia (a missionary organization dedicated to reaching the unreached billions in Asia). Over the next few weeks, the Lord confirmed to my wife and me that He was leading us to join Gospel for Asia (we will explore more about how He confirms His will in future chapters) and off we went, from Hawaii to beautiful Texas. We served on staff with G.F.A. for 10 years and by God's grace, were

---

[32] John 15:8

a (small) part of millions of people hearing the Gospel for the first time. God used a verse that talks about the call of Abraham to leave his relatives and go to Canaan, to call my wife and me to leave our relatives and go to Texas.

As far as knowing God's will on more of a daily basis, here is an example of how He might speak to you through the Bible. There may be some new responsibility that you have been asked to think about taking on. You've prayed and asked the Lord about it but you aren't sure you could do it. As you read the Bible one morning, you read, "I can do all things through Christ who strengthens me."[33] As you read those words, you know that you should accept the new responsibility and that God will help you.

Or there may be someone who has been irritating you lately. One morning or evening as you read the Bible, you read, "And be kind to one another, tenderhearted, forgiving one another, even as God in Christ forgave you."[34] You suddenly realize that even though the person that's been irritating you has been less than kind, God's will for you is to be kind, tenderhearted and forgiving toward that person and maybe even that you need to ask for their forgiveness for your attitude toward them. God speaks His

> God speaks His perfect messages to us, in His perfect timing, through His perfect Word- the Bible.

---

[33] Philippians 4:13
[34] Ephesians 4:32

perfect messages to us, in His perfect timing, through His perfect Word- the Bible.

Truth and feelings

Two men are sitting in the stands at an evangelistic crusade. The Gospel is preached and an invitation is made to come down to the stadium floor and pray to receive Jesus as Lord and Savior. Both men get up out of their seats, walk down the stairs and stand in front of the stage, and pray sincerely as the evangelist leads them. One man is weeping almost uncontrollably. He is overwhelmed by the feeling of the weight of his sins being lifted off of his shoulders. He is amazed. God has forgiven all of His sins. He feels like he is a new person. Even the colors of the grass and sky appear brighter. He knows that his life will never be the same.

The second man who listened to the message of the Gospel and prayed along with the evangelist isn't weeping. He has no feeling of a weight being lifted off of his shoulders. In fact, he doesn't feel anything out of the ordinary. He isn't amazed. He doesn't feel like a brand new person. Colors look the same to him after he prayed as they did before he prayed. He doesn't feel one bit differently than he did before he prayed. Do you think that second man is saved from his sins? He certainly may be.

Let me ask another question. If a person wins the election for President of the United States and is sworn in as President, but doesn't feel like they are the

President, are they? The answer is yes. The person is the U.S. President whether they feel like it or not.

Much of the time when we are reading the Bible, God speaks to us in a way that seems to "ring true" in our hearts. We may think, "Wow! God just spoke to me!" The Word from the Lord may pertain to something we had prayed about, were wondering about, had thought about recently, or a Word from God may be about something we hadn't even thought about but will encounter in the future. God may speak so clearly to us through the Scriptures, that we have no doubt that we have just heard from God.

On the other hand, we might read God's Word and not have any experience of a passage of Scripture "jumping off the page" at us. Like the second man at the crusade, we don't feel anything. Does that mean that God hasn't spoken a message, a rhema Word to us? Not necessarily. Many times as we read the Bible, a certain passage of Scripture may just stand out a little as we read it. We might think something like, "Hmm, I've never noticed that before." Or we might read a passage of Scripture and not even notice anything standing out to us at all.

Our God is a very gentle God[35] and He isn't prone to shouting at us through the Bible. Even when we read a passage of Scripture and don't notice anything in particular standing out to us, we should still pray about what we have read. If we seek to hear from God as we

---

[35] James 3:17

read the Bible and believe that He will speak to us,[36] we will probably be surprised by how many times we will find ourselves thinking something like, "Wow. I just read about that this morning."

When it comes to knowing God's will, we should spend time every day reading God's Word,[37] but not just reading it. We should immerse ourselves in it, seeking the knowledge, wisdom and understanding that can only come from God's Word. We also want to read it expecting to hear from God. God speaks, and we should be open to hearing Him when He does.

> **When it comes to knowing God's will, we should spend time every day reading God's Word, but not just reading it. We should immerse ourselves in it, seeking the knowledge, wisdom and understanding that can only come from God's Word.**

Some people read a chapter (or two or three) of the Bible every day. Some people spend hours every day reading. Other people read until they believe God has spoken that rhema Word to them.

There isn't a set amount of Scripture that everyone should read every day. God may lead one person to read a chapter a day and lead someone else to read two hours a day. The most important thing is to read with an open heart and mind, allowing God to speak to you through the Scriptures.

---

[36] James 1:5-6
[37] Matthew 4:4

Heavenly Father, I want to be guided by You. Help me to develop a habit of reading Your Word and as I do, please speak to me. Please give me ears to hear Your voice. Please transform my mind through the washing of the water of Your Word. Help me to be a doer of Your Word and not a hearer only. In Jesus' name, Amen.

It is extremely enriching, and many times even thrilling to have God reveal His will to us as He speaks through the Bible. As we will see in the next chapter, God clearly reveals His will to us in other ways as well.

5

O. - Observe

"...it seemed good to me..."

- Luke 1:3

If you are in a store and someone in front of you drops their wallet, what do you do? Do you walk by or do you pick up the wallet and think, "I better take this home for now. I need to pray about whether I should give it back or not?" No, you pick up the wallet and give it back to the person who dropped it. You know it's the good thing to do.

Doing what seems good

Have you ever thought about how God led the writers of the Bible to write the Bible? Luke[1] tells us how it happened for him- "Inasmuch as many have taken in hand to set in order a narrative of those things which have been fulfilled among us, just as those who from the beginning were eyewitnesses and ministers of the word delivered them to us, it seemed good to me also, having had perfect understanding of all things from the very first, to write to you an orderly account,

---

[1] While the Gospel of Luke doesn't specifically identify Luke as the author of the book, it is commonly accepted that he was, based on historical evidence.

most excellent Theophilus, that you may know the certainty of those things in which you were instructed."[2]

Luke said it "seemed good" to him. Luke wrote the book of Luke because "it seemed good" to him? Have you ever thought about that? God didn't speak to Luke with the voice of thunder and say, "LUKE, I AM YOUR FATHER! WRITE A BOOK OF THE BIBLE!" No, it just seemed like a good thing to do.

Knowing God's will is not always a powerful experience of divine revelation. Sometimes we take a look at things, think about them, and something seems like a good thing to do. That leads us to the third letter in our acronym of the C.R.O.S.S.- "O" for Observe.

Many times, we may not think of a specific Bible verse that directs us in a certain direction. We just observe the situation and we know what we should do.

As the Apostle James says, "to him who knows to do good and does not do it, to him it is sin."[3] Many times, we may not think of a specific Bible verse that directs us in a certain direction. We just observe the situation and we know what we should do.

Jesus said "...you shall love the Lord your God with all your heart, and with all your soul, and with all your mind, and with all your strength."[4] He commands us to love God with our mind. God has given us a mind and we should use our mind in loving Him.

---

[2] Luke 1:1-4
[3] James 4:17
[4] Mark 12:30

But Proverbs 3:5-6 says, "Do not lean on your own understanding…" How do we reconcile doing what seems good (which involves using our mind) with not leaning on our own understanding?

The answer is found in God's Word. God means exactly what He says. The Scripture doesn't say "Do not *use* your own understanding." It says "Do not *lean on* your own understanding." The Hebrew word that is translated as "lean" in our English language Bible is used 22 times in the Old Testament.

The word could also be translated as "rely on." It's not a light sort of "leaning." It implies more of a total reliance upon something or someone. In the book of 2nd Samuel, a young man told David (who was later to become the king of Israel) about King Saul's death. The young man said that King Saul, who had been wounded in battle against the Philistines, was "leaning on his spear."[5] The boy was saying that the spear was the thing that was keeping Saul from falling down. He was totally relying on it.

In the book of 2nd Chronicles we are told that "the children of Judah prevailed, because they relied on the LORD God of their fathers."[6] The word "relied" is the same word in the original language as that word "lean." The sons of Judah won the battle because they totally trusted in God; they were leaning heavily on Him.

---

[5] 2 Samuel 1:6
[6] 2 Chronicles 13:18

When the Scriptures tell us to "lean not" on our own understanding, it means that we should not be relying totally on our mind for our direction. At the same time, we can see clearly from Luke that there are times when the Lord leads us by allowing us to observe

> **We are supposed to use our mind but our mind should not be the main way that we are guided by God.**

certain things and we see that it would be good to do something (or on the other hand, not good to do something). We are supposed to use our minds but our minds should not be the main way that we are guided by God.

Some people might think that since Luke wrote the book of Luke because it "seemed good" to him, that he was "leaning on" his own understanding. It should probably be pointed out that Luke was a travelling companion of Paul. Paul suffered greatly for Christ on his missionary journeys and it's safe to say that since Luke travelled with Paul, he was also committed to God, and no doubt was also a man of prayer.

While there is no mention of God speaking to Luke and telling him to write the book, Luke probably prayed about it and no doubt was being led by the Holy Spirit as he observed the circumstances.

Psalm 37:4 says, "Delight yourself in the LORD; and He will give you the desires of your heart."[7] It is safe to say that the reason Luke wanted to write the

---

[7] Psalm 37:4 (NASB)

book of Luke is because God had put that desire in his heart. God then satisfied Luke's desire by allowing him to write the book. Many millions of people have been blessed because Luke wanted to do what was good. God gives each of us many opportunities to do what is good and we would be wise to keep our eyes open to see them.

Open doors

When Paul was in prison, knowing that the Lord had called him to preach the Gospel, he asked for prayer for himself and for Timothy. He wanted people to pray "that God would open to us a door for the word, to speak the mystery of Christ."[8] Many times the Lord will "open doors" for us and He wants us to use our mind to see the doors that He has opened. The Lord uses open doors to guide us into His will, as well as to confirm that He is leading us in a certain direction.

Let's say for example that you are thinking about moving to a certain city. You haven't told anyone about your possible move but you are praying about it one morning. At lunch that same day, a friend mentions that they will be going on a trip to visit that city and asks if you'd like to come along. A few days later, without knowing anything about your interest in the new city, your boss tells you that the company you work for is opening a new office in that city and offers you a job there. God opens doors.

---

[8] Colossians 4:3

As we seek to live a life of knowing God's will, we may be surprised at how often He opens obvious doors for us. It won't always be as dramatic or obvious as the example, but God wants us to know His will and sometimes He opens doors in order to help guide us. Many times, it will be in a way that causes us to think something like, "Wow. This must be the Lord."

> As we seek to live a life of knowing God's will, we may be surprised at how often He opens obvious doors for us.

Many of the doors that God opens for us aren't as easy to recognize. For example, maybe you've been wanting to visit a friend who lives a few hours travel time from where you live. You talk to your friend on the phone and find out that your friend has a few days off from work and they line up perfectly with the few days you have off from work. No fireworks or miraculous coincidences; circumstances just work out well for certain things to happen.

> God works through ordinary circumstances.

God doesn't just open big doors for us at important crossroads in our lives. He also works by opening little doors for us in our everyday life. God works through ordinary circumstances.

God will often guide us into His will by presenting opportunities for us. These may be "small" things, like saying something nice to someone, or they may be things that are more significant. We can sometimes miss God's leading by waiting to hear Him call us to China when He is wanting us to go across the street.

I attended a Christian conference in California a number of years ago. As I arrived at the conference and was getting out of my car, there was another man getting out of his car as well. It was Damian Kyle, the senior pastor of Calvary Chapel Modesto, a mega church where thousands of people attend every week. I had been introduced to Pastor Damian briefly once in the past but as far as I knew, he didn't know who I was. After all, he probably meets thousands of people in his life of ministry.

As I walked across the parking lot, Pastor Damian greeted me. He looked me in the eye and asked me how I was doing, and then listened to my answer. He paid attention to me and we spent some time talking together. I was amazed by how much he seemed to care about me. Here I am, your "average Joe" Christian, and this pastor, who no doubt, could have many important things to do, showed a genuine interest in how I was doing. He acted like I was sent from God for him to bless. I was astounded.

I doubt that as Pastor Damian drove to the conference, God spoke to him and told him to bless the guy he meets in the parking lot. No, Pastor Damian was probably just observing the opportunities that God was presenting to him to be a blessing to others. He was just doing what seemed good to him- and it impacted my life. May the Lord help us to see the thousands of "little doors" that He opens for us.

Closed doors

God also closes doors as a way to guide us. A closed

Closed doors may be blessings in disguise.

door can prevent us from going in a direction that the Lord doesn't want us to go. Let's say for example, that you'd like to get a job working at a certain store. You go to the store to apply for the job and the store manager tells you that the store is going out of business and won't be doing any more hiring. The closed door may be a blessing in disguise.

God is infinite in wisdom and knows everything. Many times we are tempted to think that God doesn't really care about us when we face a closed door, especially if we really had our heart set on something (or someone). We often think that we have all of the relevant facts and that if God would only take into account everything we know about a situation, He would surely see that we are right and would open that door for us.

When we encounter a closed door, the sooner we look at God and His character, the better. We should try to immediately think about the fact that our loving God has allowed that door to be closed. Fixing our eyes on the Lord[9] is the sure route to success and a right perspective.

God loves you and wants the best for you. He is all-knowing and perfect in wisdom. Would He keep you

---

[9] Hebrews 12:1-2

from something that is really the best thing for you? No, He wouldn't. His plans are good- every one of His plans. You can trust Him absolutely. Sometimes when the Lord closes a door, it is in order to bless us (and use us) by opening another door somewhere else.

When God closes a door, there are two possibilities: One is that He's got a better door for us to go through, and the other is that the door is only closed temporarily. It may look like a wall now but the Lord can turn it into an open door. With God, all things are possible.[10]

> When God closes a door, there are two possibilities- One is that He's got a better door for us to go through and the other is that the door is only closed temporarily.

Right door, wrong time

Maybe the timing isn't right for the door to open when we think it should. Over time, all of us will experience doors opening at just the right time and we will praise God for His perfect timing. We often think that we know best what the timing of an open door should be. Let's say for example, that you are between jobs. You've lost your previous job and you have been looking for another one but haven't been able to find one. You need money. You are willing to work, you are praying for a job and looking for employment, but you can't seem to find a job. Why, oh, why would the Lord not give you a job right away? It doesn't make sense to us. Maybe you are single and have been praying for God

---

[10] Mark 10:27

to give you a spouse but it hasn't happened. Maybe you have been waiting for years. Why wouldn't God bring you a spouse?

The closed door may even be in an area of serving God. God may be putting a certain type of ministry on your heart. You know that He's leading you to serve Him in this particular area of ministry, but He's making you wait. He's gifted you to be able to serve Him and you are willing to serve Him. Why would He make you wait rather than just opening the door right away, so that you can serve Him?

Sometimes we find out the answers to our questions as soon as the door is opened and we see that His timing is truly perfect. Other times we may not find out for years, or maybe not even in our lifetime, why God delayed a door from opening for as long as He did. In the end however, we will see that in every single situation, God's timing is perfect and His plans are perfect.

> In the end, we will see that in every single situation, God's timing is perfect and His plans are perfect.

It may be that we aren't ready to go through the door yet. There was a boy named Joseph who had a dream in which the sun, the moon and eleven stars bowed down to him. When he told his dream to his father and brothers, his father scolded him, saying ""What is this dream that you have dreamed? Shall your mother and I and your brothers indeed come to bow down to the earth before you?"[11] The dream had been given to Joseph by God. Joseph eventually became second in charge of the entire Egyptian empire but it was many years before Joseph was ready to assume such tremendous responsibility.

It was also many years before Egypt was ready for Joseph. Can you imagine how frustrating Joseph's life would have been if he had lived all those years thinking, "I'm supposed to be in charge. How come I'm not in charge? How come nobody is bowing down to me?" God is faithful and as Joseph matured and when the circumstances were just right, God opened the door.

I became a Christian when I was 30 years old. At the time, I thought that 30 was a bit older than the ideal age to get married. It was almost seven years later that I met Doreen, my beautiful bride to be. Seven years seemed like a long time to wait. If God wanted me to get married, why would He make me wait 7 years? In the year leading up to Doreen and me meeting, the Lord worked in my life and taught me some things that would help me to be a much better husband than I would have been if I had gotten married earlier. It would have been difficult for Doreen to be married to me before the Lord had prepared me for her. During those years, the Lord was working in Doreen's life as well. The timing of us meeting and getting married was perfect. We can trust God. His timing is always perfect.

---

[11] Genesis 37:10

Sometimes there are things that need to come together in order for the timing to be just right or it could simply be that the Lord wants us to learn to trust Him and to joyfully wait for His perfect timing. The testing of our faith produces patience[12] and sometimes we may have to wait for a door to open because God is wanting us to learn patience. It may be that one of the things that pleases the Lord the most, is when we wait in faith, knowing that even though we don't see an open door in front of us, we trust God and know that He will indeed give us every "good thing."[13]

Closed doors may also be a result of our hearts not being right. One of the benefits of prayer is that as we seek the Lord about a closed door, the Lord will often lead us to change how we are praying about something, in order to help us to have a right perspective about it.

James tells us that "God resists the proud, but gives grace to the humble."[14] Our pride can also be a reason that we face closed doors. We should always seek to humble ourselves before the Lord in prayer as we wait for doors to open.

Many people that you talk to who are waiting for a door to open will tell you how good their prayer times are. "I have been trying to find a job for a few months now and haven't been able to find work. God has been providing for me though, and my times with the Lord have been really good. I don't think I've ever felt as

---

[12] James 1:3
[13] Psalm 84:11
[14] James 4:6

close to the Lord as I am right now." Closed doors can be used greatly by the Lord to draw us near to Him. In fact, many times the closed doors that we think are keeping us from God's perfect will, are actually God's tools to lead us into His perfect will- His will is that we would have a close relationship with Him.

Paul had the right perspective when he said, "Yet indeed I also count all things loss for the excellence of the knowledge of Christ Jesus my Lord, for whom I have

> **Many times the closed doors that we think are keeping us from God's perfect will, are actually God's tools to lead us into His perfect will- His will is that we would have a close relationship with Him.**

suffered the loss of all things, and count them as rubbish, that I may gain Christ … that I may know Him…"[15] Paul realized that knowing the Lord was truly the best thing of all.

In some cases however, it just may be a matter of us needing to persevere in prayer about a situation. Jesus said, "knock, and it will be opened to you."[16] As we looked at earlier, the word "knock" could also be translated as "keep on knocking." As we persevere in prayer about something, the Lord may open the door for us, or lead us to change the way we are praying (and then maybe open the door). Obstacles are not a reason to give up. The Lord can open doors that are closed. If you face a closed door, pray and seek the Lord. God can

---

[15] Philippians 3:8,10
[16] Luke 11:9

guide us by closing doors but closed doors are not necessarily a "no."

Doors with difficulties

Sometimes we can mistakenly think that if we encounter trials, we must be going the wrong way. "If

> Sometimes when we face difficulties and obstacles, it's because we are doing exactly what God wants us to do.

I'm doing God's will, won't He open doors for me and make them easy to go through?" The Apostle Paul was committed to doing the will of God. While on one of His missionary journeys, he said that he would stay in a certain city, "For a great and effective door has opened to me, and there are many adversaries."[17] Wait a minute. "A great and effective door has opened" and "many adversaries?" Doesn't that sound like a contradiction? I would be tempted to say something more along the lines of, "I thought it was a great and effective door but there are many adversaries so I'd better look for another door." Difficulties are not necessarily closed doors. In fact, Paul's situation illustrates that oftentimes when we face difficulties and obstacles, it's not because God is trying to guide us away from the direction we are going; the trials and opposition are a result of us doing exactly what God wants us to do.

We have a very real enemy (the devil) and he (through his demons) fights against us as we seek to walk in God's will. Rather than be discouraged by

---

[17] 1 Corinthians 16:9

opposition, we can be encouraged, knowing that we are in God's will.

Depending on doors

The Lord can use open and closed doors to guide us but we need to be careful that we aren't reading too much into them. An old friend calls you on the phone and says, "Hey! Wanna go to a bar with me tonight?" You think, "Wow! I was just walking by the phone when they called and I didn't have

> **The danger for most of us is not that we won't observe and use our minds; it's that we would lean on our minds too much.**

any plans for tonight! What an open door!" There are many open doors that we should not go through.

Doing what seems right to us

If there is a dangerous chapter in this book, it is probably this one. Why? Because we live in a culture of leaning on our own understanding. The danger for most of us is not that we won't observe and use our minds; it's that we would lean on our minds too much. We can live our lives being led by our own reasoning, simply by doing what seems right to us.

"Every way of a man is right in his own eyes, But the LORD weighs the hearts."[18] We can always come up with reasons why we should do something that the Lord is not leading us to do, and the reasons will always sound good to us. Even when we are in rebellion, we

---

[18] Proverbs 21:2

can come up with reasons. Over and over in the Bible we are told about the trouble people got into when "everyone did what was right in his own eyes."[19]

In the Garden of Eden, Eve was deceived and disobeyed God's Word when she "saw that the tree was good for food, that it was pleasant to the eyes, and a tree desirable to make one wise."[20] Those things sound good (food, beauty and wisdom) but God had said not to eat of the fruit of that particular tree.

God's Word must always take precedence over what we may think. The book of Proverbs tells us that "The way of a fool is right in his own eyes, but he who heeds counsel is wise."[21] Or as the Psalmist writes, "How can a young man cleanse his way? By taking heed according to Your word."[22] It's very easy for us to use our minds to come up with plans that are not from the Lord, even when it comes to doing good things for God.

We can "put two and two together" and have it all figured out. We see in the Bible that God spoke to Balaam through a donkey,[23] so we think, "Hey, since God can speak through a donkey, why don't we buy a bunch of donkeys and start a donkey ministry?" While it's unlikely that anyone has used this exact line of reasoning in starting a ministry, how many of the things that we do for God are not really led by the Lord, but

---

[19] Judges 17:5-6
[20] Genesis 3:6
[21] Proverbs 12:15
[22] Psalm 119:9
[23] Numbers 22:28

are really "donkey ministries?" We start down a path without being led by the Lord and then we pray, "Please bless this, Lord."

Doing good vs. doing right in our own eyes

You might ask, "What is the difference between doing what "seems good" and doing "right in our own eyes?" Good question. Doing good involves doing what is right in God's eyes, as opposed to just doing what's right in our own eyes.

Let's say for example that you are driving down the road and someone cuts in front of you in their car.

> How many of the things that we do for God are not really led by the Lord, but are really "donkey ministries?"

You might think, "Well, if they are going to do that to me, it's only fair that I do the same thing to them. I should teach them a lesson." That might seem fair and right in our own eyes but it's not what is good in God's eyes. God says to "love your neighbor"[24] and to "overcome evil with good."[25]

As we have seen in the previous chapters of this book, we need to be committing our life to God, spending time in prayer and reading God's Word, and (as we will explore further in the next chapter) listening to the Lord. As He renews our mind and helps us to see things from His perspective, we will know what is truly good, rather than just what seems right to us.

---

[24] Mark 12:31
[25] Romans 12:21

In the book of Joshua we are told about how the men of Israel were deceived by the Gibeonites when they did what seemed right to them but "they did not ask counsel of the LORD."[26] We should observe the circumstances and use our minds to help us determine God's will, but we must not lean heavily on our own understanding. In order to know God's will, what we need more than anything is to be led by the Lord.

Heavenly Father, Thank you for being a God who guides me by giving me opportunities. Please help me to see the "Divine appointments" that you present to me, even though they may seem small at the time. Help me to know that whether it's picking up a cigarette butt or going overseas as a missionary, anything I can do to please You is a big thing. Help me to observe and to do the good things that You offer to me. In Jesus' name, Amen.

One of the greatest blessings we will experience in this life is to hear God speak to us directly. As we will see in the next chapter, our God speaks.

---

[26] Joshua 9:14

6

S. - Still, Small Voice

"And behold, the LORD passed by, and a great and strong wind tore into the mountains and broke the rocks in pieces before the LORD, but the LORD was not in the wind; and after the wind an earthquake, but the LORD was not in the earthquake; and after the earthquake a fire, but the LORD was not in the fire; and after the fire a still small voice."

- 1 Kings 19:11-12

One of the most wonderful things in the Christian life, is to experience God speaking to you. If you think about it for a minute, you can't help but get excited. The God who created the universe is willing to talk to you.

God is able to measure the universe with the span of His hand.[1] That's amazing. The size of the universe is so enormous that it's beyond our ability to fully comprehend. According to NASA, the Hubble telescope has now seen what is believed to be the most distant galaxy ever observed.[2] Travelling at the speed of light, it would take 13.2 billion years to reach this

---

[1] Isaiah 40:12

[2] http://www.nasa.gov/mission_pages/hubble/science/farthest-galaxy.html

galaxy.[3] It's hard to even grasp just how big that is. God created the vast expanse of the universe and He loves you and is willing to speak to you personally. That's awesome!

Many people think that if God spoke to someone, He would speak with a voice like thunder and that He might even cause lightning or an earthquake to occur as He spoke. In the book of 1st Kings, we are told that God spoke to Elijah with a still, small voice. God often

> God created the vast expanse of the universe and He loves you and is willing to speak to you personally.

speaks to us that way. He is gentle[4] and does not want to be forceful when He communicates with us. This brings us to the first "S" in C.R.O.S.S.- God's still, small voice.

"My sheep hear My voice"

Jesus said, "My sheep hear My voice, and I know them, and they follow Me."[5] One thing that we see in this statement is the promise that as followers of our Great Shepherd, we will hear His voice. What a precious promise; He will speak to us and we can hear Him when He does.

> We don't have to be "super spiritual" to hear from God. He wants to speak to every one of us.

---

[3] This is what NASA scientists believe, but it is not a totally proven fact. It assumes (among other things), that light has always travelled at the same speed.

[4] Matthew 11:29

[5] John 10:27

We don't have to be "super spiritual" to hear from God. He wants to speak to every one of us.

It's interesting that Jesus didn't just say, "My sheep hear My voice and they follow Me." He inserted, "and I know them." There is a sense of intimacy in "and I know them." Isn't that comforting? He knows us- sins and all. He knows everything about us and if anyone has a reason not to like us, it's Him. Yet He loves us with an everlasting love. As we looked at previously, knowing God's will involves intimacy with God and this verse (like so many other verses in the Bible) brings us back to that point.

God speaks

Some people believe that ever since the writing of the Bible was completed, the only way God has spoken to us is through the Bible. Our God is the Living God. Jesus is called "God with us."[6] He doesn't just abide with us in silence, expecting us to find verses of Scripture that deal with every situation we encounter. He not only guides and speaks to us through the Bible, He also speaks to us through His Holy Spirit. We are told in the book of Acts that "the Holy Spirit said, 'Now separate to Me Barnabas and Saul for the work to which I have called them.'"[7] Again in the book of Acts we are told, "Then the Spirit said to Philip, 'Go near and overtake this chariot.'"[8] These are both very specific messages of direction from God that resulted in many

---

[6] Matthew 1:23
[7] Acts 13:2
[8] Acts 8:29

people's lives being changed. God spoke to Christians in the early church, and He still speaks to us today.

I was walking down the street one day and the Lord spoke to me so clearly that I was amazed that it was not an audible voice. He said, "Pray!" I started praying and after walking about 50 feet further, I passed by a girl sitting in a car. I happened to have some Gospel tracts in my pocket so I held out a tract and said, "Can I give you something to read?" The girl took the tract, looked at it for a few seconds and said, "I'm definitely going to read this." She proceeded to tell me how she had just quit her job and was moving to another state to "start a new life." She said her mother had told her she needed "spiritual counsel." I was able to share the Gospel with her and she was very open to hearing it. The joy we get from being used by the Lord to help change someone's life for eternity is hard to put into words.

> God spoke to Christians in the early church, and He still speaks to us today.

There may be times when the Lord speaks to us in a "loud and clear" way, but usually He chooses to speak to us in a still, small voice. Do you want to be sensitive enough to be able to hear His voice?

Listening to God

It may seem obvious, but in order to hear someone who speaks with a soft, gentle voice, we should be listening. Many of us ask God questions but we don't give Him time to answer us. We say, "Lord, what should

I do?" and then we keep right on talking or doing something. Listening to people is a skill that needs to be developed, and so is listening to God. Many Christians wake up in the

> Listening to people is a skill that needs to be developed, and so is listening to God.

morning, spend a few minutes quickly reading a passage in a devotional book or the Bible, offer up a quick prayer (which consists of talking without listening) and then begin another busy day. It's good to spend even a few minutes with the Lord at the start of the day, but if we want to develop more of a sensitivity to hearing God's voice, we should spend more than a few minutes a day in prayer and Bible reading.

As we spend time in prayer (in the morning, evening and throughout the day) we shouldn't just talk to the Lord, we should also listen to hear what He might say to us. God will speak to us. It doesn't take hours and hours of prayer to hear from God. God can speak to us in an instant, even without us ever praying, but if we spend time communicating with Him (talking and listening), we

> If we spend time communicating with Him (talking and listening), we will become more familiar with His voice and be more open to hearing from Him.

will become more familiar with His voice and more open to hearing from Him.

Sometimes as we are seeking to know the will of God, a verse of Scripture will come to mind (especially if we regularly read and maybe even memorize Scripture). As we've already looked at, God speaks through His written word and many times the Holy Spirit will bring a Scripture to mind. We may not realize it at the time but God is speaking to us.

The 23rd Psalm is probably the most widely known passage of Scripture in the Bible. The first three verses are rich with truth when it comes to hearing from God-"The LORD is my shepherd; I shall not want. He makes me to lie down in green pastures; He leads me beside the still waters. He restores my soul; He leads me in the paths of righteousness for His name's sake."[9] King David, who wrote the Psalm, is comparing God to a shepherd and himself to a sheep.

Notice that the sheep mentioned in the Psalm isn't in a rush. He isn't running down a hill, grabbing a bite of the green grass as he flies by the Shepherd. He isn't grabbing a cup of water like a runner in a marathon running by a drinking station. He lies down in the green pastures to rest and eat, and the Good Shepherd leads him to drink "beside still waters." Then David says that his soul is restored and that God leads Him "in paths of righteousness."

Much of the time, we need to get our hearts quiet before God in order to hear from Him. We need those "still waters." We need to get away from the busy rush of life. Jesus showed us the perfect example of someone making it a priority to get alone with God to pray. He

---

[9] Psalm 23:1-3

prayed in the wilderness, on a mounain and in a garden. Even after a busy day of ministry, Jesus, "in the morning, having risen a long while before daylight, He went out and departed to a solitary place; and there He prayed."[10] He went to a quiet place and got alone with God. If we want to hear God speak to us, it's important to have a place where we can go, a quiet place where we can be alone with God (even if it means going into a closet and praying).[11]

What does God's voice sound like?

What does God's still, small voice sound like? Well, what do your thoughts sound like? God may speak thoughts into our minds. Many times that's what God's voice sounds like, except that when God speaks to us in His still small voice, it's not just our thoughts; God is actually speaking to us. I've heard it taught that God speaks to our spirit and that our spirit speaks to our mind.

> If we want to hear God speak to us, it's important to have a place where we can go, a quiet place where we can be alone with God.

If God speaking to us sounds like our own thinking, then how do we know that God is speaking to us? How do we know we aren't just imagining it, or that it isn't just our own thoughts? How do we know that it's not just "fiery darts"[12] from the evil one? Good questions, I'm glad you asked.

---

[10] Mark 1:35
[11] Matthew 6:6 (KJV)
[12] Ephesians 6:16

Jesus asked His disciples a question. He said, "Who do you say that I am?"[13] Peter responded by saying, "You are the Christ, the Son of the Living God."[14] Jesus said, "flesh and blood has not revealed this to you, but My Father who is in heaven."[15] Jesus was telling Peter that he hadn't figured that truth out by his own intellect or by some other person revealing it to him, but that God the Father had revealed it to Him. So the great truth Peter stated wasn't his idea- it was from God. This illustrates the fact that we can have thoughts in our mind that are from God, without even knowing it.

In one of Paul's letters to the Corinthians, he mentions his opinion about something and says, "and I think I also have the Spirit of God."[16] Paul is saying that he thinks that God's Spirit was agreeing with his point, but he wasn't sure. So there were times when even Paul the Apostle didn't know for sure whether an idea that he had was from God.

Have you ever said something to someone that was the perfect thing to say at that moment, and then thought something like, "Wow. Where did that come from? That must have been from the Lord." As Christians, we have the Holy Spirit dwelling in us and He speaks to us. As Paul tells us, "it is God who is at work in you, both to will and to work for His good pleasure."[17] God's Spirit is working in our lives and

---

[13] Matthew 16:15
[14] Matthew 16:16
[15] Matthew 16:17
[16] 1 Corinthians 7:40
[17] Philippians 2:13 (NASB)

sometimes God speaks to us so softly that we don't know it came from Him.

Many times however, God will speak to us and we will know that He has spoken to us. As I mentioned earlier, my wife and I served the Lord in the U.S. office of Gospel for Asia. We were a few months into serving there and I was working in the mailroom. I would often work into the night and the department that Doreen was working in would close every day at 5:00pm. She would go home and it was usually several hours before I got home. She started to make little comments about it and over time, it became a bit frustrating for her. One day she asked, "Can't you finish your work during the day and come home for dinner at a more normal time?"

The next morning in my prayer time, I asked the Lord about it. I couldn't figure it out. I was serving the Lord, helping to reach some of the most unreached people on the planet, but at the same time, Doreen was getting frustrated because I was coming home late almost every night. I prayed and asked the Lord about the situation. Then I listened for His answer. He said two things to me. The first was "Work." The second was "Love your wife."

I could have spent a lot of time trying to figure it out. How do I "balance" serving the Lord with being a good husband? Billions of people are unreached with the Gospel and I could help reach many of them but I needed to be a good husband to my wife. What God said to me cut through it all. I didn't have to try and figure out the perfect balance of being a good husband

and serving the Lord. All I had to do was walk in obedience to what the Lord said to me. As I focused on those two things- working, and loving Doreen, it was amazing how everything worked out. At the end of the day I would pray and ask the Lord when I should go home. I also asked the Lord to guide me in regard to loving Doreen and I tried to follow His leading. I don't think Doreen ever mentioned my coming home late again.

> What God said to me cut through it all. I didn't have to try to figure out the perfect balance of being a good husband and serving the Lord. All I had to do was to walk in obedience to what the Lord said to me.

Even though this happened a number of years ago, I mention it because it was a time when I believe the Lord spoke very clearly to me, and because the results were so easy to see. As I walked in obedience to His voice, I saw Him work things out in a wonderful way.

Hearing His voice isn't something that should only happen once in a while, however. It can happen every day. Just as it takes time for sheep to learn the sound of their shepherd's voice, through experience, we will get better at recognizing our Great Shepherd's still, small voice.

Learning to listen

Have you ever tried asking God what you should do on a certain day? If not, you might want to try this; during your prayer time, have a pen and paper handy and ask the Lord what you should do that day. Write down the things that come to mind. At the end of the day, look at your list. You may be surprised to see that you completed everything on your list. This can be a very encouraging way to see that you are hearing from God, especially if you compare it to what you usually get done on a day when you have your own "to-do" list.

If you write five things on the list and only two of them get done, it can help you to see that maybe at this point, you are "filling in the blanks" with your own thoughts, rather than being quiet before the Lord and allowing Him to speak to you. For many people, the idea of listening to God is a new thing. Don't be discouraged because you make mistakes, or if you don't think you are hearing anything. As you continue to surrender yourself to God in prayer and practice listening to Him, you will be amazed; God will speak to you in His still, small voice.

> As you continue to surrender yourself to God in prayer and practice listening to Him, you will be amazed; God will speak to you in His still, small voice.

From big things to beans

We don't need to ask God about trivial things like if we should sneeze or what color pants He wants us to buy. God is not a micro-manager. Many times if we seek His will about something, we won't really have a sense at all about which way He wants us to go. It may be because He doesn't really have a "perfect will" about little things such as what color pants we buy.

On the other hand, God is willing to guide us not only in the big decisions of life, but also in the little things that matter to us but that don't really matter to Him (like what color pants we buy, for example).

When Doreen and I first got married, she had only been a Christian for a short time. While seeking to disciple her, I shared with her about the fact that God is willing to guide us even in the small decisions of life. She believed me and a few days later, she went grocery shopping.

> God is willing to guide us even in the small decisions of life as we commune with Him throughout the day.

Among other things, she had green beans on her grocery list. As she looked at the green beans in the first grocery store she went to, she wondered if she should buy them or wait until she went to the next store that she was planning on going to. She prayed and asked the Lord whether she should buy the beans at the first store or the second store. She felt like He told her to wait until the second store. When she got to the second store, she saw that the green beans there were on sale.

Was it God's perfect will that she buy the green beans at the second store? Probably not; He probably didn't really care which beans she bought (and there wasn't a very big difference in price), but God was willing to guide her because He loves her and wanted to bless her (and increase her faith).

It is such a blessing to have God speak to us and He will speak not only when we are faced with big decisions, but He will speak to us even about little things throughout the day, as we commune with Him.

The umpire

The Apostle Paul says to "let the peace of God rule in your hearts."[18] This is a powerful verse in regard to knowing the will of God. The word "rule" could also be translated as "be an umpire" or "decide, determine, direct or control." God wants to guide us with His peace. Often, as we seek to know the will of God, He will give us His peace or we will feel a lack of peace about something. His peace will be like an umpire for us, leading us into His perfect will.

Let's say for example, that you are praying about helping out with the Sunday school at your church. You may have never done anything like that before, but every time you hear the announcements at church and they mention the need for people to help in the Sunday school, you think maybe it's something you are supposed to do. However, just thinking about it makes you nervous. In your prayer time one morning, you ask the Lord about it and as you pray, your nervousness about helping out is replaced by a feeling of peace. You may not hear God speaking to you but you have a peace about it. God guides us with His peace.

We should "let the peace of God rule in our hearts" not only about bigger decisions we make, but throughout the day as well. "Should I stop by and get

---

[18] Colossians 3:15

gas on my way home from work?" "Should I do the laundry today or wait until tomorrow?" The "God of peace"[19] will guide us as we seek to follow Him.

When Paul went to Troas and didn't find Titus, he said, "I had no rest in my spirit"[20] so he left Troas and went to Macedonia. God will often give us a "check in our spirit," a lack of peace about something, in order to guide us away from it. Sometimes we can't think of anything wrong with taking a certain course of action but we just don't have a peace about it. God knows everything and if He is giving you a lack of peace, you should pay attention to it. Maybe it's just a matter of timing and God will give you His peace as you continue to pray about it, but unless He does, a "check in your spirit" is a stop sign. Listen to the "umpire."

You can't make God speak

The idea of God speaking to us is very exciting. We need to keep in mind however, that we shouldn't try to force God to speak to us. He will speak to us when it is good, in ways that are good, and for good reasons.

> We shouldn't try to force God to speak to us. He will speak to us when it is good, in ways that are good and for good reasons.

Like many people, I have been blessed by going on prayer walks. I spend some time in the morning praying (and reading the Bible) and then go for a walk. While I'm walking, I will sing to the Lord and try to allow

---

[19] 1 Thessalonians 5:23
[20] 2 Corinthians 2:13

Him to lead my times of praying. One morning as I walked along, I prayed, "Lord, please speak to me; whatever You want to say to me or want me to pray about." I continued walking along and as I walked, I didn't sense the Lord putting anything on my heart. I started singing to the Lord again and then asked Him again to speak to me. More silence. The Lord didn't seem to be saying anything to me. I worshipped the Lord some more and asked Him again to speak to me. After what seemed like a while, the Lord finally spoke to me. He said, "I just want to be with you." I was shocked. God wants to be with me? Yes, and He wants to be with you, too.

Prayer is not just about talking to God and having Him talk to us. It's about spending time with God. He loves us and just as we would want to spend time with someone we love, God wants to spend time with us.

What listening to God is not

Many people who are into Eastern mysticism will repeat a word or phrase over and over until they reach an altered state of consciousness. They do this in order to empty their mind so they can hear "the universe," or their "spirit guides." Some Christians will do the same thing in order to hear from God. Jesus warned against using "vain repetitions" in prayer like "the heathen do."[21] We don't need to (and shouldn't) chant something over and over in order to hear from God.

---

[21] Matthew 6:7

How do we know when it's not God?

Sometimes when God speaks to us, we aren't sure whether or not we are hearing from Him. However, there are ways to know when God is definitely not speaking to us.

> **If you are thinking that the Lord is leading you to do something that the Bible says is wrong, then you are mistaken about His leading. The Bible is the standard by which we can measure all things.**

For one thing, God would never tell us to sin. It's amazing how many people blame their sins on God. They lie, cheat or steal and then say, "Oh, God told me to do that." God created the whole universe but one thing He didn't create is sin. One of the wonderful things about the Bible is that Scripture tells us very clearly, what is, and what is not, sin. If you are thinking that the Lord is leading you to do something that the Bible says is wrong, then you are mistaken about God's leading. The Bible is the standard by which we can measure all things.

Secondly, God is always right. He never makes a mistake. If you think He has told you something about a particular situation or person and it turns out not to be true, then it wasn't God's still, small voice speaking to you.

Let's say for example, you are thinking about buying strawberries at a certain store but don't know if they have them in stock. You pray and ask God, "If I go to the store now, will they have strawberries?" If you think that the Lord said "Yes" but you go to the store and they don't have any strawberries, you can know that you weren't hearing from God. As Jesus said, He is "the Truth" and He never makes mistakes.

Speaking of mistakes, there are many people who claim to be prophets. They say they are speaking for God. Well, if they prophesy one thing about current or future events that isn't true or doesn't come to pass, or doesn't line up with what the Bible says, you can know they are false prophets.[22] All it takes is one false prophecy. The Bible tells us about those who are deceived in their hearts who prophesy falsely,[23] saying that God told them something when He really didn't. God takes it very seriously. In Old Testament times, God dealt with false prophets very severely; "But the prophet who presumes to speak a word in My name, which I have not commanded him to speak, or who speaks in the name of other gods, that prophet shall die."[24]

"God told me…"

Many times when God speaks to us, it's not "loud" enough for us to be able to say, "God said. . ." We believe that we are hearing from Him about something but we aren't absolutely sure. God knows what's best for us and it would be quite easy for us to become very prideful if we were hearing lots of "messages from

---

[22] Deuteronomy 18:22
[23] Jeremiah 14:14
[24] Deuteronomy 18:20

God"[25] and we were to walk around telling people, "God told me this…" and "God told me that…" We could get quite puffed up with pride. Maybe that's one reason why God doesn't always speak to us in a way that we can definitely say, "God said. . ."

There are some people who say they are hearing from God when they aren't. Have you ever heard someone say something like "God told me…" and then go on to tell you all kinds of zany things that the Lord supposedly told them. Sometimes they will tell you about long conversations they have with God. You might wonder if the additives in the pepperoni on their pizzas are affecting their thinking. Or you think, "How come they have these great conversations with God but I don't? I must be spiritually inferior."

God is the same yesterday, today and forever,[26] and if He wants to have a conversation with someone, He can. Sometimes however, when people say "God told me. . .," they either have an over active imagination or they are deceiving you in order to impress you with their "spirituality."

> The fact that people make counterfeit money is no reason for us to stop using real money. In the same way, the fact that people abuse the idea of God speaking to people shouldn't keep us from seeking to hear from God.

The fact that people make counterfeit money is no

[25] 2 Corinthians 12:7
[26] Hebrews 13:8

reason for us to stop using real money. In the same way, the fact that people abuse the idea of God speaking to people shouldn't keep us from seeking to hear from God, and of course, sometimes when people say, "God told me. . ." or "God said. . .," they are telling the truth.

The wisdom of Daniel and Mary

It's noteworthy to see how some people in the Bible responded when they received a message from the Lord. In many cases, you don't read of those who heard from God, rushing out to tell everyone that God had spoken to them. The book of Daniel details some amazing revelations from God. It's interesting that Daniel didn't always immediately tell people that God had spoken to him or what God had revealed to him. After he received one of his most amazing revelations from God, he didn't run out and tell everyone about it. Instead, he said "but I kept the matter in my heart."[27]

Mary, the mother of Jesus, also had some amazing things revealed to her by God. The angel Gabriel told her she was going to give birth to the Son of God. It's noteworthy that there is no mention in the Bible of Mary telling anyone that an angel of God had spoken to her, telling her she would be the mother of Jesus. When Jesus was born, shepherds came into town and told people about how the Angel of the Lord appeared to them and told them that the Savior was born, "but Mary kept all these things and pondered them in her heart."[28]

---

[27] Daniel 7:28
[28] Luke 2:19

Like Daniel, Mary didn't run out and tell everyone that God had revealed great things to her.

There are definitely times when we should tell others about things we believe the Lord has spoken to us. Sometimes the Lord may tell us something in order for us to tell it to someone else. God wants us to be ambassadors for Christ.[29]

Many times however, the Lord speaks to us in order to guide and bless us. He is not pleased by our boasting to others about Him speaking to us. As the Apostle James tells us, "So then, my beloved brethren, let every man be swift to hear, slow to speak…"[30]

This is the way

One of the most amazing and wonderful experiences of the Christian life is having the Lord speak directly to you. God is willing to speak to us not only about big decisions and at important crossroads in our life, but every day, throughout the day. Our God is the God who says, "Your ears shall hear a word behind you, saying, 'This is the way, walk in it,' whenever you turn to the right hand or whenever you turn to the left."[31]

God wants to reveal His will to us. As we seek to listen to the Lord when He speaks, and as we walk in obedience to what He tells us, we will get better at

---

[29] 2 Corinthians 5:20
[30] James 1:19
[31] Isaiah 30:21

hearing His voice. Throughout the day, ask the Lord for direction, seek to listen to God's voice and let the peace of God rule in your heart. Will we make mistakes? Of course, sometimes we will think the Lord has said something to us but it was just our own thoughts. However, as we continue to fellowship with God and practice listening to Him, we will get better and better at knowing when He is speaking to us. Jesus is "God with us"[32] and it is such a wonderful truth that

> **Jesus is "God with us" and it is such a wonderful truth that He isn't just with us in silence- our God speaks.**

He isn't just with us in silence- our God speaks.

Heavenly Father, Thank you for being a God who speaks. Jesus, You are the Great Shepherd. Please give me a sensitivity to Your voice and discernment to know when I am hearing from You. I want to know Your voice and to follow You. Help me to get in the habit of not only talking to You, but listening as well. In Your name I pray, Amen.

As we will see in the next chapter, God sometimes reveals His will to us by speaking to us in an audible voice; the voice of a brother or sister in Christ.

---

[32] Matthew 1:23

7

S. - Saints

"Where there is no counsel, the people fall; but in the multitude of counselors there is safety."
- Proverbs 11:14

We like the idea of Almighty God speaking to us directly. That's exciting. Sign me up. I want to know the will of God and I like the idea of hearing it straight from Him. But having to listen to people? What if I don't like listening to people? You may have heard people who serve in Christian ministry joking about it and saying, "Ministry would be great if it weren't for the people." This brings us to the second "S" in C.R.O.S.S.- Saints.[1]

The reality is that the church of God is not a building with people in it and it's not an organization. It's an organism- a body.[2] As Christians, we are the body of Christ. When I first became a Christian, I got the idea in my mind that I was going to do great things for God. Yup, it was God and me. I was excited about the future. What was I going to do for God? What wonderful things would I be able to accomplish for His glory?

---

[1] As followers of Jesus, God calls us "saints."- See 1 Corinthians 1:2
[2] 1 Corinthians 12:13

It took a long time for me to realize how God works when it comes to following Him. For years, I couldn't understand why Jesus would say "By this all will know that you are My disciples, if you have love for one another."[3] What I thought He should have said was something like, "By this all will know that you are My disciples, by the great things you do for Me." Jesus said exactly what He meant to say.

People see that we are His followers and people are drawn to Christ when we love each other. You don't often see a "lone ranger" Christian that God uses to accomplish much for His Kingdom. God delights in working through the body of Christ.

So what does this have to do with knowing God's will? God compares Christians to a human body[4] for good reasons. As members of the body of Christ, we are interdependent. Just as your kidneys and lungs wouldn't function without the rest of your body, and your body wouldn't function without your kidneys and lungs, so each of us is designed to be a part of the body of Christ and He uses us to help each other to know His will. Can you imagine someone's elbow saying, "I can figure this thing out. I don't need the spine and nervous system to help me."?

> God compares Christians to a human body for good reasons. As members of the body of Christ, we are interdependent.

---

[3] John 13:35
[4] 1 Corinthians 12:4-27

God speaks through God's people

The Apostle Paul is a great example of how God guides us into His perfect will by using other believers. When Paul first turned to Christ on the Damascus road (at that time he was called "Saul"), he said, "Who are You, Lord?" Then the Lord said, "I am Jesus, whom you are persecuting."[5] Jesus was speaking directly with Saul. Saul asked Jesus, "Lord, what do You want me to do?" Jesus didn't say, "It's you and Me, Saul. You are going to be an Apostle and you will take all your orders directly from me." No, instead, He said to him, "Arise and go into the city, and you will be told what you must do."[6] Jesus directed Paul to do what he was told to do by another Christian. Jesus was talking to Paul, face to face. Why didn't the Lord just tell Paul what He wanted him to do? Because God delights in working through the body of Christ. Right from the beginning of Paul's relationship with Jesus, He wanted Paul to know that sometimes God leads us through other Christians and He wanted Paul to humble himself and take direction from another person.

Over time, Paul grew in His knowledge of God and in his usefulness to God. He was chosen by God to be one of the Apostles, the leaders of the early church. He eventually impacted hundreds of millions of people's lives for Christ through his leadership and writing of at least 13 books of the New Testament.

---

[5] Acts 9:5
[6] Acts 9:6

It is interesting to note that even after Paul had become a leader in the church, there were times when God's will was revealed to him through other people.

During one of Paul's missionary journeys, he was in the city of Ephesus and wanted to go into a theater to preach the Gospel. People in the theater were in an uproar because of the impact the Gospel was having on the local idol making industry. The disciples didn't think it was a good idea for Paul to go into the theater. "And when Paul wanted to go in to the people, the disciples would not allow him. Then some of the officials of Asia, who were his friends, sent to him pleading that he would not venture into the theater."[7] Paul didn't go into the theater and he left the city of Ephesus.

> It is interesting to note that even after Paul had become a leader in the church, there were times when God's will was revealed to him through other people.

You would think that if there was anyone who would know the will of God without having to listen to other Christians, it would be Paul. He was an Apostle. He didn't just know the Scriptures, he wrote 1/3 of the New Testament! Yet God spoke to him through other believers. It's one of the ways the Lord reveals His will to us.

Even Chrisitan leaders need to be willing to listen to what other believers have to say. None of us are

---

[7] Acts 19:30-31

exempt. There are times when even young children can say things that can help us to discern the will of God.[8]

Who should we listen to?

"Blessed is the man who walks not in the counsel of the ungodly."[9] Nobody likes drinking water from a dirty cup, and the cleaner the cup, the easier it is to taste the water. It's the same when it comes to hearing from the Lord through people. If we want to taste the pure water of God's word, to hear clearly through someone what the will of the Lord is, then we want to find people who are like a clean cup. We want to listen to people who love the Lord, have an intimate relationship with Him, have a good prayer life, and are walking in obedience to Him- people who really know the Lord.

> If we want to taste the pure water of God's word, to hear clearly through someone what the will of the Lord is, then we want to find people who are like a clean cup.

These people may be Christians who know you well and really care about you. As King Solomon said, "As iron sharpens iron, so a man sharpens the countenance of his friend."[10] I can't begin to count the number of times that the Lord has led me into His will through the counsel of other believers. Again, from King Solomon, "in a multitude of counselors there is safety"[11] and

---

[8] Matthew 21:16
[9] Psalm 1:1
[10] Proverbs 27:17
[11] Proverbs 24:6

"Listen to counsel and receive instruction, that you may be wise in your latter days."[12]

Sometimes however, people who are close to you may not be the best ones to listen to when it comes to God's will for your life. Why? In the days leading up to His crucifixion, Jesus began to tell the disciples that He would be mistreated by the religious leaders, be killed and then rise again on the third day. "Then Peter took Him aside and began to rebuke Him, saying, 'Far be it from You, Lord; this shall not happen to You!' But He turned and said to Peter, 'Get behind Me, Satan! You are an offense to Me, for you are not mindful of the things of God, but the things of men.'"[13]

Even though our friends and family members want what is best for us, at times they can be more concerned with what they think is good for us, than they are with what God wants. They "are not mindful of the things of God, but the things of men."

> **We want to listen to mature believers who have God's interest at heart, rather than people who will just tell us what they think we want to hear or what they think will benefit us.**

We want to seek counsel from people who are willing to tell us the hard truth; "Faithful are the wounds of a friend. . ."[14] We want to listen to mature believers who have God's interest at heart, rather than people who will just tell us

---

[12] Proverbs 19:20
[13] Matthew 16:22-23
[14] Proverbs 27:6

what they think we want to hear or what they think will benefit us.

Along those lines, we want to go to brothers and sisters in Christ who will pray and listen to the Lord. What a treasure we have in people who will do that for us.

Fellowsheep

The Bible makes it abundantly clear that God wants us to gather together as Christians. "And let us consider one another in order to stir up love and good works, not forsaking the assembling of ourselves together, as is the manner of some, but exhorting one another, and so much the more as you see the Day approaching."[15] God uses people not only to love,[16] encourage,[17] teach,[18] rebuke,[19] and pray for us,[20] but also to exhort us, to call us to come along side of them in following the Lord.

There are more than 50 verses in the New Testament alone that reveal God's will for us in regard to how we should treat "one another," that is, other Christians. As we walk in obedience to His word; loving and fellowshipping with Christians, we will be amazed at how God uses other believers to help us to know His good and perfect will for our lives. This doesn't just mean attending church. We need to spend time

---

[15] Hebrews 10:24-25
[16] John 13:34
[17] 1 Thessalonians 3:2
[18] Colossians 3:16
[19] Luke 17:3
[20] James 5:16

fellowshipping, interacting and sharing our lives with other Christians. This can't be accomplished in the two minutes of time after a pastor says, "Let's turn and greet one another." We need to be more like those first century Christians who "continued steadfastly"[21] in fellowship. How this works in your life may be different than how it works in someone else's life. As you seek the Lord about it, He will guide you as to how you can please Him by regularly fellowshipping with other Christians. This is an important part of living a life of knowing the will of God.

What about leaders?

We live in a rebellious culture. We don't like being told what to do. We want to be the captains of our own ships. Then Christ comes into our lives. We come to the place where we admit that God is God and we're not. (I like what I once read on the back of a T-shirt, "There is a God and you're not Him.") So we receive Jesus as our Lord and Savior and we surrender to Him. We're happy to have Him leading our life. Then we read or hear a verse like Romans chapter 13, verse 1- "Let every soul be subject to the governing authorities," and we think, "I wish God hadn't put that in the Bible." Even after becoming a Christian, our human nature doesn't like people telling us what to do.

God tells us to submit ourselves to the governing authorities. It wouldn't honor God for you to be

---

[21] Acts 2:42

standing in a courtroom in front of a judge, saying, "Well, your honor. I felt the Spirit of God leading me to drive 65 miles per hour in a 55 mile per hour zone and to run that red light." The judge might answer back, "Well, I feel the Spirit of God leading me to fine you $240.00 for speeding and $351.00 for running the red light."

We don't have to seek the Lord to determine whether it's God's will for us to break the law whenever we want to. The Bible tells us to submit to governing authorities unless what the governing authority wants us to do violates God's Word.[22]

When a parent tells their child to take out the trash, the child can know what God's will for them is. God wants them to take out the trash. We know this because God's Word says, "Children, obey your parents in all things, for this is well pleasing to the Lord."[23]

> When a parent tells their child to take out the trash, the child can know what God's will for them is. God wants them to take out the trash.

Wives should submit to the leadership of their husbands.[24] We know this is God's will because God's Word says it is. (Of course, husbands should listen to

---

[22] Acts 5:29
[23] Colossians 3:20
[24] Ephesians 5:22

their wives. Men can miss God's will by not listening to the concerns and the godly counsel of their wives.)[25]

God gives us leaders in the church as well, and He gives wisdom and revelation to pastors and other Christian leaders. Christians should take counsel and direction from Christian leadership.[26] We can easily miss the will of God because we are not willing to follow the spiritual leadership that God has set up in our lives.

> **Christians so often miss the will of God because they are not willing to follow the spiritual leadership that God has set up in their lives.**

As we seek to know the will of God, it's amazing how often we will be listening to our pastor or another Bible teacher, and we will receive direction from the Lord. You may be praying about something and then in church or while listening to a Christian radio broadcast, God speaks to you.

A pastor may mention during the message (or afterwards in conversation) that he didn't know why he mentioned a certain thing, but in fact it was exactly what you needed to hear in order to know God's will. God speaks through people and we should be open to hearing from Him when He does.

Regardless of what type of human authority it is, God is the final authority. When a human authority directs us to do something that goes against God's

---

[25] Genesis 21:12; 31:16
[26] Hebrews 13:17, 1 Thessalonians 5:12-13

Word, we should always submit to God, rather than people.

What about unbelievers?

God can do anything He wants to do, including speaking through non-believers. He spoke to the prophet Balaam through a donkey. God can speak through donkeys, but let's not line them up to give us direction. Non-chrisitans are not donkeys, but Balaam's donkey demonstrates that

> God can speak through donkeys, but let's not line them up to give us direction.

even though God can speak to us any way He wants too, it is important to seek God's will in ways that He directs us to. The Bible warns us against following the counsel of unbelievers[27] and it's surprising how often Christians will seek counsel from them. It's also surprising how often their advice will be along the lines of, "You've got to think of yourself…"

When I first turned to Christ, I mentioned to a non-Christian family member that I had become a Christian. She said, "Not one of those 'Born Again' ones I hope?" Not wanting to disappoint her, I gave a rather vague reply, "Well, some people might call it 'born again.'" Her response surprised me, "You either are or you aren't!" she said. I was forced to decide. "Well then, in that case, I am." I replied. I don't know for sure but I believe that the Lord may have put it on her heart to

---

[27] Psalm 1:1

question me. He wanted me to be willing to take a stand for Him, to be willing to "confess Him before men."[28]

There are times when the Lord may use what an unbeliever says to us. Of course, not everything an unbeliever says is wrong. An unbeliever may even quote a passage of Scripture that is just what we need to hear at just the right time. While God can definitely use unbelievers to guide us, the direction from the Bible is clear; we should not be seeking direction from unbelievers in order to follow the Lord.[29]

Quick to hear

As we seek to know the will of God, it is a tremendous blessing to have God speak to us through people. Many times they will have no idea that the message coming from them is precisely what we need to hear. Rather than being resistant to hearing what the will of God is through other believers, we should be "quick to hear,"[30] eager and open to how the Lord might speak to us through another member of the body of Christ; just as we are eager to hear the Lord speak to us through His written Word or His still, small voice.

> We should be "quick to hear," eager and open to how the Lord might speak to us through another member of the body of Christ.

---

[28] See Matthew 10:32
[29] Psalm 1:1
[30] James 1:19 (NASB)

Like a parent who loves to see their children helping one another, God loves to see us blessing each other by coming alongside, helping and encouraging one another to walk in His perfect will.

Heavenly Father, Thank you for giving me other Christians to help me to know Your will. Please help me to be devoted to fellowshipping with other believers so that I might encourage them and be encouraged by them in walking with You. Help me to be "quick to hear" what You want to say to me through other believers and to submit to the leaders that You have brought into my life. In Jesus' name, Amen.

Sometimes as we seek to know the will of God, He seems to be silent. We want to know His will but He doesn't seem to want to tell us which way to go. As we will explore in the next chapter, God has some very good reasons for making us wait.

8

Waiting and Persevering

"I wait for the LORD, my soul waits, and in His word I do hope."

— Psalm 130:5

God is able to do "exceedingly abundantly above all that we ask or think."[1] That's amazing. Then why does it sometimes seem like He's either unable to hear us, or not willing to answer when we ask Him to reveal His will to us? Sometimes He makes us wait. Most of the time, He doesn't say, "Wait." We just don't hear anything. Why does God make us wait?

Waiting and waiting

In the United States, we live in a country that's in a rush, and things seem to be getting busier. We are proud of ourselves if we are able to do several things at once and we want to get better at it. A few years ago, you never heard the word "multitasking." Now you hear it often. People used to talk about taking time to "smell the roses." Now we drive by them so fast, we don't even see them. Proverbs 19:2 says, "…it is not good for a soul to be without knowledge, and he sins who hastens with his feet." That verse is rich with truth for

---

[1] Ephesians 3:20

all of us who live in these busy times. The two "not good" things mentioned in that verse are connected; being without knowledge and rushing.

When you think about Noah's ark, you can't help but be impressed at what Noah accomplished for God. The ark was about 450 feet long and about 75 feet wide. That's one and a half football fields in length. Building the ark must have been a tremendous task. It's interesting to note however, that Noah didn't start building the ark until he was about 500 years old. What does the Bible say Noah did before that? He "walked with God."[2] God wanted to do a great work through Noah- once he turned 500. The Lord is not usually in the rush that we can so easily be in.

We should be "zealous for good works."[3] The word "zealous" could also be translated as "boiling hot." We should be on fire to serve God, but in order to know God's will and live a life that is pleasing to Him, it is vital that we are people who have an intimate relationship with God. Like Noah, we want to be people who "walk with God."

Part of that intimacy involves waiting on Him. We can't always have everything all figured out when we want to. God created the seasons and He is a God of perfect timing. "The eyes of all look expectantly to You, and You give them their food in due season."[4] God will

---

[2] Genesis 6:9
[3] Titus 2:14
[4] Psalm 145:15

not only guide us into His perfect will, He will guide us at the perfect time.

People come up with all kinds of sayings, like this one; "God can't steer a parked car." In other words, "If you don't know what God wants you to do, just start doing something for Him, and then He will guide you." The saying is intended to "stir up

> **God will not only guide us into His perfect will, He will guide us at the perfect time.**

love and good works,"[5] which is good. For many of us, our "car" needs to get moving. We are saved "for good works,"[6] and many times we need to be taking the first steps of obedience to the Lord before He will give us the next steps, but serving God isn't a substitute for seeking God's will. When I hear someone say, "God can't steer a parked car," I'm tempted to say, "Cars need to pull into gas stations sometimes for fuel and directions," although I guess a more Biblical response would be, "Where there is no vision, the people perish."[7]

> **If we want to live a life of knowing God's will, we have to be willing to do more than work. We have to be willing to wait.**

If we want to live a life of knowing God's will, we have to be willing to do more than work. We have to be willing to wait. The Prophet Isaiah tells us, "But those who wait on the LORD shall renew their strength; They shall mount up with wings like eagles, They shall run

---

[5] Hebrews 10:24
[6] Ephesians 2:10
[7] Proverbs 29:18 (KJV)

and not be weary, They shall walk and not faint."[8] Not only do we receive direction from the Lord as we wait on Him, but also the spiritual strength to serve Him.

Prepared soil

Just as a farmer prepares the soil before planting seeds, sometimes God wants to do a work in our hearts to prepare us for what He will be leading us into. There may be things in our life that we need to fully surrender to the Lord before we are ready to go where He wants to lead us. As we wait on the Lord, we should seek to draw near to the Lord with our whole hearts, and we should try to be sensitive to the Lord as we pray in order to be led by the Holy Spirit. Sometimes as we do that, He'll guide us to pray about things in ways that we hadn't prayed before, and then lead us in directions that we hadn't even considered. This can be an exciting part of our walk with the Lord- seeing things in new ways and being led by Him into new things.[9]

> Not only do we receive direction from the Lord as we wait on Him, but also the spiritual strength to serve Him.

As we wait on the Lord to guide us and then see how He guides us time after time, we learn to trust Him. Trusting in the Lord can be a tremendous source of peace for us. Rather than leaning on our own understanding, we patiently wait for Him. And as we looked at earlier, trusting in Him with all of our heart is

---

[8] Isaiah 40:31
[9] Isaiah 43:19

a key to knowing His will. As we trust in Him, He will direct our path.[10]

As we wait for God's direction, it's important for us to keep in mind that God is the goal. He is the prize. There is nothing better than Him. "Draw near to God and He will draw near to you."[11]

Perseverance

In 1831, Abraham Lincoln failed in business. In 1832, Lincoln lost when he ran for the state legislature. In 1833, Lincoln failed again in business. In 1835, Lincoln's fiancée died. In 1836, Lincoln had a nervous breakdown. In 1843, Lincoln lost when he ran for the U.S. Congress. In 1848, Lincoln lost again when he ran for the U.S. Congress. In 1855, Lincoln lost when he ran for the U.S. Senate. In 1856, Lincoln ran for U.S. Vice President; he lost. In 1859, Lincoln lost again when he ran for the U.S. Senate. In 1860, Abraham Lincoln was elected the 16th President of the United States of America. People accomplish the most amazing feats as they persevere against all obstacles. They endure incredible trials, climb the highest mountains, swim across raging rivers, and go faster, deeper, higher, longer and farther than anyone else- because they persevere.

Seeking and serving

If we want to be people who know and do God's will, we need to be people who persevere; in both

[10] Proverbs 3:5-6
[11] James 4:8

seeking and serving the Lord. The Bible gives us many examples of men and women of faith who persevered and as a result, were able to fulfill God's perfect will for their lives.

The Apostle Paul endured tremendous persecution and hardship for the Lord, including beatings, a stoning, imprisonment, shipwrecks, nights without sleep, hunger and thirst.[12] Paul was willing to persevere. In his letter to the Philippians, he wrote, "Not that I have already attained, or am already perfected; but I press on, that I may lay hold of that for which Christ Jesus has also laid hold of me."[13]

> If we want to be people who know and do God's will, we need to be people who persevere; in both seeking the Lord and in obedience to His leading.

Paul "pressed on." He persevered and toward the end of his life, he wrote, "I have fought the good fight, I have finished the race, I have kept the faith."[14]

One of the keys to finishing any race is to stay on course. If you're watching a marathon and see one of the runners veer off course and head into an "all you can eat" buffet restaurant, you don't have much hope that he or she is going to finish the race very well. We must be willing to persevere in the area of seeking the Lord, as well as in the area of obedience to His leading. We see from Paul's life that he was a man who followed the leading of the Lord. He stayed on course. He was

---

[12] 2 Corinthians 11:23-29
[13] Philippians 3:12
[14] 2 Timothy 4:7

willing to endure hardship for the Lord. As the writer of Hebrews tells us, "let us run with endurance the race that is set before us."[15]

Of course, the ultimate example is Jesus. He came down from Heaven to do God's will[16] and even said that His "food," what He lived on, was doing the will of God.[17] We often hear about the ultimate sacrifice that Jesus made for us and

> **Knowing God and doing His will, should be more important to us than anything else on earth.**

the heart of a servant that Jesus had when He was on the earth, but there is another aspect of Jesus that doesn't always get mentioned- His zeal. He was radically committed to doing God's will. Jesus was so zealous that it even resulted in Him being alienated from his own brothers and sisters.[18] While none of us wants to be alienated from our family members, knowing God and doing His will should be more important to us than anything else on earth.

Through the prophet Isaiah, God calls Jesus, "My servant."[19] In fact, the entire Gospel of Mark presents Jesus as the perfect Servant. Jesus said, "the Son of Man did not come to be served, but to serve, and to give His life a ransom for many."[20]

---

[15] Hebrews 12:1
[16] John 6:38
[17] John 4:34
[18] Psalm 69:8-9
[19] Isaiah 42:1
[20] Mark 10:45

Jesus came to earth in order to serve. He was passionate about doing God's will and yet when He mentions serving God, it's helpful to look at the context of His statements about it. He said, "The first of all the commandments is: 'Hear, O Israel, the LORD our God, the LORD is one. And you shall love the LORD your God with all your heart, with all your soul, with all your mind, and with all your strength."[21] Notice that He mentioned loving God with all of our heart, before He mentioned loving God with all of our strength. Again, Jesus said, "You shall worship the LORD your God, and Him only you shall serve."[22] Notice again that worship is mentioned before service. We want to be on fire to serve God but *the fire comes from our close relationship with Him.* Intimacy with God is not only our source of guidance; it's our source of strength.

> **Intimacy with God is not only our source of guidance; it's our source of strength.**

Small beginnings

It is a wonderful thing to want to serve the Lord. Some of us even want to do great things for God. As I mentioned previously, when I was a new Christian, I got the idea in my mind that I wanted to do great things for God. I was hoping that somehow Billy Graham would find out that I existed, and would call to ask me to join him in preaching the Gospel to thousands of people in

---

[21] Mark 12:29-30
[22] Matthew 4:10

stadiums. Guess what happened? That's right. He never called me.

Sometimes we can be looking for God to guide us into doing great works for His glory. He might just want us to pick up cigarette butts, clean toilets or take out the trash. Are you willing to take out the trash for the glory of God?

The Apostle Paul, who accomplished amazing things for the Kingdom of God said, "Whether you eat or drink, or whatever you do, do all to the glory of God."[23] Whether God is leading us to serve Him by picking up a piece of trash in a parking lot, teaching Sunday school, or preaching the Gospel to millions, it is all an incredible privilege. Being able to please the God who created the universe is a blessing far beyond anything we deserve.

God spoke to Zerubbabel and told him to rebuild the temple of God that had been destroyed.[24] As Zerubbabel and the people worked on the foundation of this second temple (which consisted of moving rocks around), people noticed that it looked like nothing in comparison to the temple that had been built previously. God responded by saying, "For who has despised the day of small things?"[25] As we serve the Lord faithfully in little things, God will often give us "bigger" things to do for Him. We should be "zealous

---

[23] 1 Corinthians 10:31
[24] Haggai 1:1-15
[25] Zechariah 4:10

for good works,"[26] whether they are little things or great works for God.

What if the Lord only wanted you to do "little things" for Him? Would you be willing to do them? When we get to Heaven, we will be rewarded for our faithfulness to what God asked us to do. I don't want to be standing

> What if the Lord only wanted you to do "little things" for Him. Would you be willing to do them?

in front of the Lord saying, "Look, Lord. I built a Fortune 500 company," and have Him say, "But I wanted you to teach Sunday school."

Go with what you know

As the Lord leads us, He will often give us just enough information for us to be able to take the next step, and we need to be willing to take it. We may not know why He is leading us in a certain direction. We may not know what we will be encountering as we go forward, either. At one point in his journeys, Paul said, "And see, now I go bound in the spirit to Jerusalem, not knowing the things that will happen to me there, except that the Holy Spirit testifies in every city, saying that chains and tribulations await me."[27] Paul knew that the Lord was leading him to Jerusalem, and he knew that he would encounter "chains and tribulations," but beyond that, he didn't know what would happen to him. Paul willingly went forward, knowing that God was leading

---

[26] Titus 2:14
[27] Acts 20:22-23

him, and knowing that God's plans are good. You and I need to be willing to go forward and follow the Lord's leading, even if we don't know where we are going.[28]

God will often lead us into things without giving us the whole picture. As we obey and persevere in faith, we please God by showing that we trust Him. At the same time, we develop the habit of depending on Him and seeking Him at every step.

God repeats Himself

What if you think that the Lord is leading you in a certain direction but you aren't sure? It might involve a fairly big decision on your part. You don't want to take a chance and just jump into something that may be a wrong decision. The Lord knows what we need. In those times when we need confirmation to be sure that He is leading us in a certain direction, as we continue to seek Him and wait on Him, the Lord will repeat Himself so that we can know for sure.

We've looked at how the Lord reveals His will to us in a variety of different ways. Many times God will guide us into His will by communicating to us more than once. He may speak to us a certain way several times, or through more than one method.

When I met Doreen and soon thereafter started praying about marrying her, I didn't want to get it wrong and miss God's leading in my life. I needed to know if it was His will for us to get married. I became

---

[28] Hebrews 11:8

very emotionally attached to Doreen, but I didn't want my personal feelings for her to get in the way of my hearing from the Lord. (As we will explore later in the book, our personal bias can easily hinder us from discerning the will of God.)

I got a sheet of paper and started to write down how I thought the Lord was guiding me in regard to marrying Doreen. God is faithful and by the time I asked Doreen to marry me, I had a page and a half of journaling. Through the Bible, open doors, God's still, small voice and other believers, God made it abundantly clear that it was His will for us to get married. I didn't have to guess and then hope that I got it right.

We're in a war

Picture someone walking through a field of flowers. It's a beautiful sight. The person stops to smell one of the flowers and as they lean over, a bomb explodes just a few feet from where they are standing. Then another bomb explodes as bullets blaze by, but the person in the field is oblivious to what is going on around them. In a war, the worst place to be, is on the battlefield without knowing you are in a war.

According to a recent Barna survey, only about half of the adults in the U.S. that could be described as "born again Christians" strongly believe that the devil is real.[29] That means that about half of American Christians don't really believe that the devil and demons

---

[29] www.barna.org, April 10, 2009

exist and that we are in a war with them. The Bible is very clear that spiritual forces of wickedness do in fact exist; whether people believe they do or not. In the book of Ephesians, we are told to "Put on the whole armor of God, that you may be able to stand against the wiles of the devil. For we do not wrestle against flesh and blood, but against principalities, against powers, against the rulers of the darkness of this age, against spiritual hosts of wickedness in the heavenly places."[30]

The passage of Scripture goes on to describe the "armor of God" that we have for our spiritual battles, and then exhorts us to be "praying always with all prayer and supplication in the Spirit, being watchful to this end with all perseverance..."[31] Sometimes there is a need to persevere in prayer because of our enemy. Of course, we don't need to be afraid of the powers of darkness, since "He who is in you is greater than he who is in the world."[32]

The devil is a defeated enemy and he will soon be thrown into the lake of fire where he will be for eternity. Currently however, he and his demons are trying to hinder the work of God and His people, and prayer is a vital weapon in our battles against him. As we persevere in prayer, we will see breakthroughs. As the Apostle James tells us, "The effective, fervent prayer of a righteous man avails much."[33]

---

[30] Ephesians 6:11-12
[31] Ephesians 6:18
[32] 1 John 4:4
[33] James 5:16

Slow down and fast

It's wonderful to read verses in the Bible where God speaks clearly to people. "While they were ministering to the Lord and fasting, the Holy Spirit said, 'Set apart for Me Barnabas and Saul for the work to which I have called them.'"[34] When you read this verse, did you notice that seven letter word- "fasting"?

We want to know the will of God and we are willing to do His will, but what if at times, we need to fast in order to hear from Him? Are we willing to pay the price? "Personally, I wouldn't mind fasting if I just didn't get so hungry when I was doing it." "My body hates fasting." "My metabolism doesn't seem well suited for fasting." "Fasting makes me irritable." "I get hungry too quickly." I've heard all of those excuses; from myself! The reality however, is that there are many benefits of fasting and one of them is that fasting is a powerful tool to help us to hear from God.

> **We want to know the will of God and we are willing to do His will, but what if at times, we need to fast in order to hear from Him? Are we willing to pay the price?**

Jesus prophesied about His friends, saying, "But the days will come when the bridegroom will be taken away from them, and then they will fast in those days."[35] Jesus is "the bridegroom" and He has been taken away. He said that His friends (we are His friends) would fast.

---

[34] Acts 13:2 (NASB)
[35] Mark 2:20

One of the most widely known passages of Scripture is what is referred to as "The Lord's prayer" in Matthew, Chapter 6, where Jesus tells His disciples how to pray. It's interesting that immediately after telling His disciples about prayer, Jesus said, "Moreover, when you fast..."[36] Notice that He didn't say, "Moreover, *if* you fast."

Fasting is a form of self-denial. It denies our own will in order to pursue spiritual things. Most fasting involves not eating any food, or not eating certain foods. I once heard of someone "fasting" from a certain well known coffee shop. That might not really be fasting.

Fasting is not a way to somehow force God into answering our prayers, or of forcing Him to speak to us. It is however, a way to experience victory over our flesh. King David said, "I humbled myself with fasting."[37] It is also a way to gain victory over spiritual opposition.[38] It is a powerful weapon in spiritual warfare. The Prophet Daniel fasted and prayed for 21 days until the angel Michael broke through the opposition of "the Prince of the kingdom of Persia"[39] so that Daniel could receive a revelation from God.

Making fasting a part of your life can help you to know the will of God. When fasting, it's important not only to limit food intake, but even more importantly, to

---

[36] Matthew 6:16

[37] Psalm 35:13 (See also 1 Kings 21:27-29)

[38] Matthew 4:1-3; 17:18-21 (See also Isaiah 58:6)

[39] Daniel 10:13

spend time in prayer. If you don't spend time in prayer when you are fasting, all you will get is hungry.

There are different ways to fast. Some people skip a meal or two a week (and spend the time praying, that they would have spent preparing and eating their meals), or fast for a day every week or once a month.

> If you don't spend time in prayer when you are fasting, all you will get is hungry.

Some people go on "Daniel fasts," eating only vegetables and fruit, and drinking only water.[40] Ask the Lord to guide you in fasting and you will soon see the blessings that it brings as you seek to know the will of God.

Visions and dreams

Sometimes God reveals His will to us through a vision or a dream. The prophet Joel spoke of the time in which we are now living, saying, "Your old men shall dream dreams, your young men shall see visions."[41] God may give you a dream or a vision, whether or not you are seeking His will about something in particular. It may be during a time of fasting, or it may be when you aren't fasting.

Paul was "forbidden by the Holy Spirit to preach the word in Asia"[42] and then "a vision appeared to Paul in the night. A man of Macedonia stood and pleaded with him, saying, 'Come over to Macedonia and help

---

[40] Daniel 1:12, 10:2-3
[41] Joel 2:28
[42] Acts 16:6

us.""[43] Based on his vision, Paul concluded that the Lord was calling him to preach the Gospel to the Macedonians.

God is sovereign and can do whatever He wants to do, whenever He wants to do it. We shouldn't be surprised by God occasionally guiding us through a supernatural event such as a dream or vision.

Heavenly Father, Thank You for being a God who will use the times of waiting in my life. Help me to persevere in waiting, in serving, and in praying. Help me to be faithful in the "little things" that You want me to do. In Jesus' name, Amen.

There are some other reasons why God is silent when we are seeking to know His will, and as we will see in the next chapter, these reasons have nothing to do with God wanting us to wait.

---

[43] Acts 16:9

9

Hindrances to Hearing

"Behold, the LORD's hand is not shortened, that
it cannot save; nor His ear heavy, that it cannot
hear."

- Isaiah 59:1

Good news, bad news

Sometimes when we seek to know the will of God,
it seems like someone has a hearing problem- either
God or us. We can't discern what His will is. Why won't
He guide us so that we can know which way to go? As
we looked at in the previous chapter, God may want us
to wait and persevere, but there are also a number of
other things that can keep us from being able to discern
the will of God. The bad news is that we are the reason
for these obstacles. The good news is that we can
overcome every one of them.

Leaving our first love

The greatest commandment is to love the Lord with
all of our "heart, soul, mind, and strength." Notice that
loving God starts with our hearts. When we drift away
from that priority, things start to fall apart. It's easy for
us to lose our ability to discern God's will if our focus is
wrong. The Psalmist writes, "Do not be like the horse

or like the mule, which have no understanding, which must be harnessed with bit and bridle, else they will not come near you."[1] God's desire is that we would "come near" to Him. That's more important to the Lord than anything else we could do. If we start to drift away from loving God, our spiritual life will become dry and monotonous and we will lose our motivation for doing God's will.

In order to know God's will, it is critical that we are "looking unto Jesus,"[2] loving Him, worshipping Him and thanking Him. There are many verses in the Bible telling us to give thanks to God. It's interesting to note that two of the things mentioned about the unrighteous in relation to God are that they don't "honor Him as God or give thanks."[3] It is so easy for us to take our many blessings for granted and to neglect to give God thanks, and yet thanksgiving is one of the best ways to draw near to God. As we spend time thanking God, we find ourselves worshipping and loving Him. We need to regularly reflect on who God is, what He has done, what He is doing and what He will do. Truly, God is worthy of our love, worship and thanksgiving. Needless to say, spending time in prayer and reading the Bible are also important elements to help us maintain our

> If we start to drift away from loving God, our spiritual life will become dry and monotonous and we will lose our motivation for doing God's will.

---

[1] Psalm 32:9
[2] Hebrews 12:2
[3] Romans 1:21 (NASB)

intimacy with God and to keep us from leaving our "first love."[4]

Prayerlessness

This may be one of the most important paragraphs in this book. Scripture says that we should be "continuing steadfastly in prayer"[5] or as another translation reads, we should be "devoted to prayer."[6] Considering that the average time spent in prayer every day by American Christians is about 5 minutes, it's no wonder that many

> When it comes to spending time with God in prayer, the quality of time we spend with Him is more important than the quantity of time.

people have a hard time developing a sensitivity to the Lord's voice. Of course, when it comes to spending time with God in prayer, the quality of time we spend with Him is more important than the quantity of time.

It's a matter of the heart, and what we each need is an intimate relationship with God. In a relationship between two people, "quality time" is more likely to happen when there is a good quantity of time being spent together. In the same way, we can have a more intimate relationship with God if we are willing to spend time with Him in prayer. An undeveloped prayer life is one of the biggest reasons people have a hard time knowing God's will.

---

[4] Revelation 2:4
[5] Romans 12:12
[6] Romans 12:12 (NASB)

As Christians, every one of us has a relationship with God. He is our Heavenly Father.[7] We will have that relationship whether we spend time in prayer or not. Spending time with the Lord in prayer doesn't make you any more a child of God than you are right now. What prayer gives you (among other things) is fellowship with God.

When the "prodigal son" left home,[8] his *relationship* to his father didn't change. He never stopped being his father's son, but his *fellowship* with his father was severed. The difference between many Christians is not in their relationship with God; it's in their fellowship with Him.[9]

We can miss out on so much and live our lives in our own strength rather than the Lord's strength, simply because we don't make prayer a priority in our lives. "Unless the LORD builds the house, they labor in vain who build it."[10] You can do all kinds of things and have them be for nothing. As we spend time with the Lord in prayer, not just talking, but also listening; we get to know Him better, we become familiar with the sound of His voice, and we become much more sensitive to His leading. Are you willing to set your alarm clock to wake you up earlier in order to spend an hour a day in prayer

> A life that is devoted to God is a life that is devoted to prayer.

---

[7] John 1:12
[8] Luke 15:11-32
[9] 1 John 1:3
[10] Psalm 127:1

(or whatever amount of time the Lord puts on your heart)? Prayer can radically change your life for the better.

Sin

There is only one thing that separates us from God- our own sin. Sometimes as we seek to know God's will and can't seem to receive His guidance, it's because there is sin in our life and we need to repent (change our mind about it). "Behold, the LORD's hand is not shortened, that it cannot save; nor His ear heavy, that it cannot hear. But your iniquities have separated you from your God; and your sins have hidden His face from you, so that He will not hear."[11] When we won't turn from our sins, the issue is not that God *can't* hear us; it's that He *won't* hear us. He is Holy and Righteous and when we are living in sin, we are in effect, pushing God away from us.

> There is only one thing that separates us from God- our own sin.

Part of committing our life to the Lord is continually coming before Him in prayer, asking Him to reveal to us any sins that we need to confess to Him. We should pray along the lines of King David, who prayed, "Search me, O God, and know my heart; Try me, and know my anxieties; and see if there is any wicked way in me, and lead me in the way everlasting."[12] When we ask the Lord to speak to us about any sins

---

[11] Isaiah 59:1-2
[12] Psalm 139:23-24

that we need to confess to Him, and we listen to Him, He will bring things to mind. It's wonderful that, "If we confess our sins, He is faithful and just to forgive us our sins and to cleanse us from all unrighteousness."[13] When we confess our sins to God, He not only forgives us but He cleanses us and helps us to resist the temptation to commit those sins again.

Pride

Some of us are proud of our pride. We can come up with all kinds of reasons why pride is ok (by blaming it on our nationality, for example). That's too bad since, "Pride goes before destruction, and a haughty spirit before a fall."[14] The Bible is very clear on the subject of pride. God didn't create pride; the devil did, and we are warned about the danger of being puffed up with pride and falling into "the same condemnation as the devil."[15]

It is very easy for us to harden our hearts because of our pride. God warns us about those who harden their hearts, saying, "'Therefore it happened, that just as He proclaimed and they would not hear, so they called out and I would not listen,' says the LORD of hosts."[16]

Pride comes naturally to us and we so often don't see it in ourselves. It's something that we need to turn from and confess to God every time it rears its ugly

---

[13] 1 John 1:9
[14] Proverbs 16:18
[15] 1 Timothy 3:6
[16] Zechariah 7:13

head. "God resists the proud, but gives grace to the humble."[17]

In the Book of Isaiah, God tells us where He dwells; "For thus says the High and Lofty One Who inhabits eternity, whose name is Holy: 'I dwell in the high and holy place, with him who has a contrite and humble spirit.'"[18] God dwells with the humble and we want Him to dwell with us, so we should seek to walk in humility before Him. We should heed Peter's admonition-"Therefore humble yourselves under the mighty hand of God, that He may exalt you in due time."[19] As we spend time worshipping God, reading the Bible, and acknowledging who He is, it helps us to have a right perspective and to humble ourselves. Compared to God, "Behold, the nations are as a drop in a bucket, and are counted as the small dust on the scales."[20] I don't think that verse is referring to a whole lot of dust, either- just a light coating of dust- "small dust." Compared to the greatness of God, that's what the nations are- small dust. We should keep that in mind. We should walk in humility before God.

Taking offense

John the Baptist was the forerunner to Jesus and God spoke powerfully through John as he preached repentance in preparation for the coming of the Lord. He told people that he wasn't worthy to even carry the

---

[17] 1 Peter 5:5
[18] Isaiah 57:15
[19] 1 Peter 5:6
[20] Isaiah 40:15

sandals of Jesus.[21] John proclaimed that Jesus was "The Lamb of God who takes away the sin of the world,"[22] and "the Son of God."[23] Things changed however.

Around the time that Jesus began to preach about the Kingdom of God, John was imprisoned for speaking out about the sins of King Herod. Jesus didn't do anything to get John released from prison, and it offended John. He sent two of his disciples to ask Jesus, "Are You the Coming One, or do we look for another?"[24] Do we look for another? This is after John had been telling people that Jesus was the Son of God. Now he's in prison, saying in effect, "What's up with this? You are "the Son of God" but you won't do anything to get me out of prison?! Are you really Him?!"

We can be like John. We know who Jesus is. He's God. He died for our sins. He's amazing. Then when something happens that upsets us, we get offended at Him. Jesus' response to John is for us as well. He reminded John that He had fulfilled numerous prophecies that only the Messiah would be able to fulfill, and then He said, "And blessed is he who is not offended because of Me."[25] One of the reasons we can take offense at the Lord is because, like John the Baptist, we can have unrealistic expectations about how things should happen in our life. We need to be careful that we don't take offense at the Lord when things don't

---

[21] Matthew 3:11
[22] John 1:29
[23] John 1:34
[24] Luke 7:19
[25] Luke 7:23

go the way we think they should. When we are offended, we need to repent and ask the Lord to forgive us and cleanse us from our pride.

Unrealistic expectations

When Jesus mentioned how Peter was going to die, Peter asked about John, saying, "'But Lord, what about this man?' Jesus said to him, 'If I will that he remain till I come, what is that to you? You follow Me.' Then this saying went out among the brethren that this disciple

> We need to be careful not to take offense at the Lord when things don't go the way we think they should.

would not die. Yet Jesus did not say to him that he would not die, but, 'If I will that he remain till I come, what is that to you?'"[26] So the disciples took what Jesus said and made it into something more than what He meant. As a result, they had unrealistic expectations about what would happen. This can happen to us so easily. We take something that the Lord says and change it into something that He didn't mean. Then when our expectations aren't met, we become discouraged and lose faith in God. We blame it on God, but it's not His fault, it's ours, beause we had unrealistic expectations.

> We need to be very careful to listen to exactly what the Lord says and not to add to it in our minds. God means what He says and our expectations should be based on God's Word.

---

[26] John 21:21-23

We need to be very careful to listen to exactly what the Lord says and not to add to it in our minds. God means what He says and our expectations should be based on God's Word.

Impatience with God

God's timing is not always the same as our timing. We often think that we know when God should move His mighty hand, whether it's in revealing His will to us, or in any other situation. He knows everything and His plans are good. As we learn to wait on the Lord, we can experience a tremendous amount of peace, rather than going through the stress that we can so easily put ourselves through. "I wait for the LORD, my soul waits, and in His word I do hope."[27] "Be anxious for nothing, but in everything by prayer and supplication, with thanksgiving, let your requests be made known to God; and the peace of God, which surpasses all understanding, will guard your hearts and minds through Christ Jesus."[28]

A number of years ago, I was standing in line at a bank and I started to get impatient. "Why couldn't this line move faster?" I decided to stop "waiting" in line. Instead, I started to pray for people in the line and for others as well. Instead of stress, I felt peace. I then decided that I would never "wait" in a line again. Rather than waiting, I would pray. That decision has brought me a real sense of peace, hundreds and hundreds of

---

[27] Psalm 130:5
[28] Philippians 4:6-7

times (and I'm sure that lives have been changed by God answering those prayers as well). Every time I realize that I am waiting, it is a reminder for me to pray.

Being biased

When we have strong feelings about something, it can easily cloud our ability to hear God when we are seeking to know His will. Let's say for example, that someone asks you to go somewhere that you don't want to go. When you ask the Lord whether or not you should go, you don't really want to hear what He will tell you. You in effect, pray something like, "Lord, Do you want me to go? No or no?" When we feel strongly about something, our own thoughts seem to almost yell in our mind and can keep us from hearing the Lord's still, small voice.

> When we have strong feelings about something, it can easily cloud our ability to hear God when we are seeking to know His will.

This is a very important obstacle to overcome as we seek to know the will of God. No matter how strongly we feel about something (or someone), we need to surrender it to the Lord in prayer. We may need to surrender something to the Lord a number of times before we have completely given it to Him.

Jesus set the perfect example of surrender on the night before He was betrayed, arrested and taken away to be crucified. He knew He would experience incredible agony and prayed, "O My Father, if it is possible, let this cup pass from Me."[29] But Jesus was totally committed to His Heavenly Father. He wanted to do God's will at any cost. He prayed, "Father, if it is Your will, take this cup away from Me; nevertheless not My will, but Yours, be done."[30] He fully surrendered Himself to doing the will of God.

Whenever we are seeking God's will about something that we have strong feelings about, we need to surrender it to the Lord in prayer. As we do, it will free us to be able to hear what the Lord will say to us.

Balance vs. obedience

We all want balance in our life. We know for example, that it is good to work hard, and we know that we also need rest. God set the example for us in the creation of the Universe. He worked six days and then rested on the seventh.

Balance can be a good thing, but we need to be careful not to let the idea of "balance" get in the way of something that is far more important; our obedience to God. It's very easy to use "balance" as an excuse to not allow Jesus to really be the Lord of our life. Whether we realize it or not, we come up with a rule that runs our life. Sort of like a "statement of purpose." Something that makes us feel "good enough." It might be something like, "I'll go to church on Sundays. I'll try to be a good person and I'll read the Bible sometimes."

---

[29] Matthew 26:39
[30] Luke 22:42

It may seem like we have balance in our life but that sort of thinking can keep us at a distance from God. Our relationship with God will tend to be on our terms rather than according to His plans. Instead of being led step by step by the Lord, we live our life as a routine established by our own understanding. Our life can be led by "balance" rather than obedience, and by routine rather than relationship.

Let's say a family member or friend says to you, "Hey, would you like to check out the home fellowship?" Instead of taking a moment to allow the Lord to speak to you about it, you respond with, "Oh, thank you, but I think Sunday mornings are enough for me." We can prevent ourselves from knowing and doing the will of God when we become content in the routines we have set up in our lives.

How do we free ourselves from the natural tendency to live in "balanced" routines? We surrender to God; not just once, but on a continual basis. We keep coming back to Him over and over again, praying as Jesus taught us to pray, "Thy will be done…" We strive to be a "living sacrifice" and we find victory through our continual surrender.

Balance is not the key to knowing God's will- intimacy and surrender are. Our goal shouldn't be to live a life of balance- it should be to live a life of worship and surrender.

> **Balance is not the key to living a life of knowing God's will- intimacy and surrender are.**

The fear of man- What will people think?

The Lord may lead us in directions that are contrary to what some people think are the best plans for us. Whether it involves taking a job or quitting a job, where to live, where to fellowship, whether to marry, who to marry, getting involved in ministry for the Lord, or any other decision, some people may not think we are making the best choice. If we believe that the Lord is leading us in a certain direction, we must be willing to go in that direction even if it doesn't make sense to other people. We need to be willing to say, "I am doing this because I believe this is what God is leading me to do."

Whether our decisions involve spiritual matters or not, we don't want to be considered a fanatic or a "Jesus freak." We don't want people to think that we are getting "carried away" with this "being led by the Lord" thing. Why is that? It's because we want to be accepted by other people. The Bible tells us that "the fear of man brings a snare."[31] We can be so concerned about what people think of us, that we end up missing God's will. Instead of acknowledging God, we make decision after decision based on what other people will think of us. It's an easy trap to fall into and oftentimes we don't realize we've become ensnared.

Jesus came to "seek and save that which was lost"[32] and He said, "Follow me and I will make you fishers of

---

[31] Proverbs 29:25
[32] Luke 19:10

men."[33] As we seek to live a life of doing God's will, we will see that God will give us an increasing desire to be used by Him to help people come to know Jesus. As we step out in obedience to the Lord in seeking to win people to Christ, we will often face opposition.

People laugh it off when they see someone so fanatical about a football team that they walk around with a plastic piece of cheese on their head or wearing a football jersey. But if we are in a conversation with someone and we mention what the Bible says, many people will see us as fanatics or idiots.

When people around us act in an ungodly way and we don't participate with them, we may be ostracized. When people ask us to lie or commit other sins and we refuse, they may call us "prude" or "self-righteous." When we mention "God" or the name "Jesus," they may think we are "kooks."

If we want to live a life of knowing God's will, we must be willing to pay the price of rejection and ridicule. In fact, we should rejoice when we are persecuted for the Lord's sake. Jesus said, "Blessed are those who are persecuted for righteousness' sake, For theirs is the kingdom of heaven. Blessed are you when they revile and persecute you, and say all kinds of evil against you falsely for My sake. Rejoice and be exceedingly glad, for great is your reward in heaven, for so they persecuted the prophets who were before you."[34]

---

[33] Matthew 4:19
[34] Matthew 5:10-12

The fear of man- What will people do?

Doing the will of God will cost you. In many countries, the price that people pay to follow Christ is a lot higher than it is in the U.S. People may lose their homes, possessions, and even their children. They are imprisoned (sometimes for many years), beaten, tortured, and even killed for following the Lord.

> Whether it's losing our lives or the respect of our friends, there is a very real price to pay for following Jesus.

In the U.S., it's rare that someone is beaten or killed for Christ. We might lose friends, relationships with family members or coworkers, and maybe even our jobs, but we generally pay a far lower price for being a Christian than many Believers around the world. But whether it's losing our lives, or the respect of our friends, there is a very real price to pay for following Jesus. As Paul tells us, "all who desire to live godly in Christ Jesus will suffer persecution."[35] We should be willing to pay any price for Him who gave everything, and suffered and died for us.

Heaven is a much better place than this earth. We are going to have eternal rewards for our faithful obedience to our King. It will be joy beyond our wildest dreams.[36] Rather than fearing what people can do to us, "let us lay aside every weight, and the sin which so easily ensnares us, and let us run with endurance the race that is set before us, looking unto Jesus, the author and

---

[35] 2 Timothy 3:12
[36] 1 Corinthians 2:9

finisher of our faith, who for the joy that was set before Him endured the cross, despising the shame, and has sat down at the right hand of the throne of God. For consider Him who endured such hostility from sinners against Himself, lest you become weary and discouraged in your souls."[37] We should be willing to do the will of God; no matter what the cost.

Needing to know why

Our natural tendency is to want God to explain things to us in advance. We want the 10 or 20 year plan for our lives, or at least the 3 month plan. "If you'll just explain why you want me to do this Lord, I'll happily do it." However, more often than not, the Lord leads us one step at a time. He desires for us to walk intimately with Him, and to trust Him.

For example, some afternoon, the Lord might put it on your heart to go for a walk. You believe that you are hearing from the Lord but you don't know why He wants you to go for a walk. You might pray, "Where do you want me to walk to, Lord?" You seek to listen to the Lord but He seems to give no response. "Hmm, silence," you think. "I guess it's not the Lord putting it on my heart to go for a walk." So you don't go for the walk. You won't know how the Lord might have wanted to bless you and use you if you had only obeyed and stepped out in faith.

---

[37] Hebrews 12:1-3

God will often lead us without giving us reasons why; sometimes leading us to do things that don't make sense to us, or others. How about when God told Philip to go to the desert?[38] At the time when Philip was told by an angel to go to the Gaza desert, God was pouring out His Spirit in Samaria. God was performing miracles as Philip told people about Jesus, and multitudes were responding to the Gospel.[39] Why would God tell Philip to go to the desert of Gaza? Why in the world should Philip leave?

There is no record of God giving Philip any reasons why He was leading him to the desert. No, God was leading Philip one step at a time. After Philip had completely obeyed God by taking the first step, then God gave Philip the next step. As he travelled along, Philip saw a man in a chariot. "Then the Spirit said to Philip, 'Go near and overtake this chariot.'"[40] The man had great authority and was in charge of the treasury of Candace, the Queen of the Ethiopians. As Philip ran to the chariot, he heard the man in the chariot reading a prophecy about Jesus, in the book of Isaiah. Philip was able to lead the man to Christ and as a result, there were probably many other people who also came to Christ as the Gospel spread to Ethiopia.

We shouldn't expect to always understand why the Lord is leading us in a certain direction. If we expect Him to give us the whole picture before we are willing

---

[38] Acts 8:26
[39] Acts 8:5-6
[40] Acts 8:29

to step out in obedience, we will miss so much of what the Lord has for us. The Apostle Paul tells us, "We walk by faith, not by sight."[41] God often gives us just enough information to guide us into taking the first step. When we obey Him and complete the first step, then He will guide us into taking the next step.

> **If we expect God to give us the whole picture before we are willing to step out in obedience, we will miss out on so much of what the Lord has for us.**

In Hebrews chapter 11, we are told, "By faith Abraham obeyed when he was called to go out to the place which he would receive as an inheritance. And he went out, not knowing where he was going."[42] Those can be words of tremendous encouragement to us; "He went out, not knowing where he was going." Abraham didn't know the whole plan, but He obeyed God in what the Lord was leading him to do. It's the same for us, we may not know the future but we know the God who holds the future, and that's what matters.

Jesus said, "Therefore do not worry about tomorrow, for tomorrow will worry about its own things. Sufficient for the day is its own trouble."[43] In many cases, if we knew all of the difficulties that lay ahead of us

> **We may not know the future, but we know the God who holds the future, and that's what matters.**

[41] 2 Corinthians 5:7
[42] Hebrews 11:8
[43] Matthew 6:34

as we take a certain path, we might not be willing to take that path, but the Lord knows what we can handle and how He is going to help us through our difficulties. We don't need to worry about the future; we just need to walk closely with Him, and be obedient to His leading.

Lord, Thank you for loving me so much, that You were willing to die for me. Help me to stay close to You. I want to know Your will and I don't want to stray from You. Help me to be quick to repent of sin and to stay in the place where Your peace is truly ruling in my heart. In Your name I pray, Amen.

What happens when we've already gotten it wrong- very wrong? We want to know the will of God but we've already walked so far away from it, so many times, that it seems like we've missed our chance. In the next chapter, we'll look at what happens when we make wrong decisions and miss the perfect will of God.

10

Wrong Decisions

"Now the word of the LORD came to Jonah the second time, saying. . ."

- Jonah 3:1

Jonah missed the boat

You may feel like you got to where you are now by making dozens or even thousands of wrong decisions. And here you are, reading the second to the last chapter in a book about doing the will of God and you are wondering if there is a place for you in God's perfect plan.

God said to Jonah, "Arise, go to Nineveh. . ."[1] But Jonah got on a ship heading to Tarshish, which is in the opposite direction. It's like being told to go to New York, but heading to Los Angeles instead. All of us make wrong decisions- lot's of them. Sometimes, like Jonah, we make wrong decisions on purpose, and sometimes we make them by mistake. Either way, it's sin. It's missing the mark. Like Jonah, we miss the boat. Maybe you feel like you've missed the boat so many times, you don't even know where the dock is anymore.

---

[1] Jonah 1:2

In Romans 8:28, we are told that "…all things work together for good to those who love God, to those who are the called according to His purpose."[2] That is a wonderful promise. God causes all things to work together for the good for those who love God. What that verse does not say however, is that "God causes all things." (So we can't blame our sins on God.) Or that "God causes all things to be good." (Sin is never good.) He does cause all things to work together for our good however, and we can draw tremendous hope from this promise.

> "…all things work together for good to those who love God, to those who are the called according to His purpose." - Romans 8:28

Disobedience

Let's say that a man lights a fire and it burns his neighbor's house to the ground. If the man confesses his sin to God, God will forgive him. He is such a merciful God. When Peter asked Jesus, "'Lord, how often shall my brother sin against me, and I forgive him? Up to seven times?' Jesus said to him, 'I do not say to you, up to seven times, but up to seventy times seven.'"[3] Jesus didn't want Peter to start counting the number of times that his brother sinned against him and stop forgiving him when it reached 490 times. Jesus was telling Peter to have a heart of forgiveness- to forgive over and over and over again. Why? Because that's the heart of God. He is so incredibly merciful. He doesn't

---

[2] Romans 8:28
[3] Matthew 18:21-22

add up our sins and say, "Uh, oh. That's strike three. You're out!" No, God has a heart of forgiveness and when we confess our sins to Him, He separates them from us as far as the east is from the west.[4] You can travel east forever and never be going west. When we sin and then turn and confess our sins to God, we aren't disqualified- we're forgiven.

> God doesn't add up our sins and say, "Uh, oh. That's strike three. You're out!"

Bad results

The man who burned down his neighbor's house and confessed his sin to God is forgiven, but the neighbor's house is still burned down, and the neighborhood still smells like smoke. Even though God forgives us, there are results of sin. As we saw in the life of Joseph,[5] many years of suffering resulted from Joseph's brothers' sins. Joseph's brothers suffered, Joseph's father suffered, and Joseph suffered.

God told Jonah to go to Nineveh, but Jonah disobeyed God and got on a ship heading to Tarshish. God sent a storm that was so severe; the ship Jonah was sailing on was almost destroyed.[6] The men on the ship feared for their lives and threw the ship's cargo overboard to lighten the ship so that it wouldn't sink. Jonah's rebellion resulted in everyone on the ship going

---

[4] Psalm 103:12
[5] Genesis 37-50
[6] The fact that God sent the storm shouldn't make us think that God's ways aren't good. Because of Jonah's rebellion, the storm was necessary in order to bring about Jonah's repentance and the eventual salvation of the entire city of Nineveh.

through a lot of hardship. In addition to that, Jonah was swallowed by a great fish and spent three days and nights in its stomach. After three days of being in the dark, sitting in fish guts, Jonah finally repented and prayed to God.

Good results

When Jonah prayed, the Lord spoke to the fish and it vomited Jonah onto dry land. "Now the word of the LORD came to Jonah the second time, saying, 'Arise, go to Nineveh, that great city, and preach to it the message that I tell you.'"[7] Those words speak volumes about the grace of God- "Now the word of the LORD came to Jonah the second time." God didn't give up on Jonah. He still used him to accomplish His will in preaching to the people of Nineveh. The Ninevites repented and were spared from God's judgment. In fact, even the men who were on the ship with Jonah while he was in rebellion, "feared the LORD exceedingly, and offered a sacrifice to the LORD and took vows."[8]

> It's always better to choose obedience to God but it's wonderful to know that even when we have disobeyed, God can and will still use us to accomplish His will if we turn to Him and make the choice to walk in obedience.

Jonah could have made the choice to do God's will when the Lord first spoke to Him. He chose the hard way instead. There is a price to pay for disobedience. We can learn that the easy way or the hard way. It's

---

[7] Jonah 3:1-3
[8] Jonah 1:16

always better to choose obedience to God, but it's wonderful to know that even when we have disobeyed, God can and will use us to accomplish His will, if we turn to Him and make the choice to walk in obedience. "For a righteous man may fall seven times and rise again."[9]

I didn't know

Maybe disobedience to God isn't what you think has brought you to where you are now. Maybe you are thinking, "I haven't really been running away from God's will, like Jonah was, but I have been "leaning on my own understanding" for so long that I must be way off track from where God wanted me to be. I think I have missed out on God's will for my life."

> Do you feel like you've missed the boat to Nineveh because you didn't know that God wanted you to get on it, and now here you are, living in Tarshish?

Do you feel like you've missed the boat to Nineveh because you didn't know that God wanted you to get on it, and now here you are, living in Tarshish?

Our God is the God who knows the beginning from the end. He knew that you would be reading this right now. He's not up in Heaven wringing His hands and saying, "Uh, oh. How in the world did you end up way over here?" God loves you and His plans for you

---

[9] Proverbs 24:16

are good. Nobody on earth has followed God perfectly, except for Jesus. We all fall short and God has always known we would fall short. He is not sitting up in Heaven, wondering how He can get you all the way back to where He wants you to be.

Before God created the Universe, He knew every single sin that you and I would ever commit. Did that stop Him from loving us? No. He sent His Son to die for us. Paul (formerly "Saul") was persecuting Jesus[10] and the early Christians. He stood guarding the clothing of those who were stoning Stephen (the first martyr of the church) to death.[11] It's safe to say that Saul was very far away from God's perfect plan for His life. But Saul surrendered to the Lord and God was able to use him to accomplish amazing things for the Kingdom of God.

The Apostle Paul knew that he fell short and said "This is a faithful saying and worthy of all acceptance, that Christ Jesus came into the world to save sinners, of whom I am chief."[12] There is no doubt that every one of us has messed up- a lot. Paul called himself the "chief" of sinners and yet he said, "but one thing I do, forgetting those things which are behind and reaching forward to those things which are ahead, I press toward the goal for the prize of the upward call of God in Christ Jesus."[13]

---

[10] Acts 9:4-5
[11] Acts 7:58
[12] 1 Timothy 1:15
[13] Philippians 3:13-14

Whether you think you have missed God's will because of your disobedience, your ignorance, or both, our God is the God who said, "So I will restore to you the years that the swarming locust has eaten. . ."[14] God spoke this to the children of Israel who had sinned and walked away from His perfect plans for them. Not only did

> Today should not just be a sad day for you as you reflect on how you got off track. It should be an exciting day. You can walk closely with the God who loves you, and you can know and do His will.

He promise restoration of what sin had brought about, but He promised them, "You shall eat in plenty and be satisfied, and praise the name of the LORD your God, who has dealt wondrously with you."[15]

That's God's heart. He wants to guide, bless and use you for His glory. He is the God who said, "Behold, all things have become new."[16] Today should not just be a sad day for you as you reflect on how you got off track. It should be an exciting day. You can walk closely with the God who loves you, and you can know and do His will.

Heavenly Father, Thank You for loving me. I have sinned so many times that I can't even begin to count them, and yet You have chosen to show me mercy. Thank You for forgiving me and cleansing me from my sins. Thank You for being a God who understands my weaknesses. Before You made the universe, You

---

[14] Joel 2:25
[15] Joel 2:26
[16] 2 Corinthians 5:17

knew how many times I would sin and yet You chose to love me anyway. Thank you. Please guide me into Your perfect will for my life. In Jesus' name, Amen.

In the beginning of this book, we looked at the fact that knowing the will of God starts at the cross. In the next chapter, we come full circle and see that knowing the will of God ends at the cross as well.

Conclusion-

It Ends at the Cross

"If anyone desires to come after Me, let him deny himself, and take up his cross daily, and follow Me."
- Luke 9:23

A life of knowing and doing the will of God is a life of peace and joy- peace and joy that no amount of money can buy, no one can steal, and that is just a taste of the good things God has in store for us in Heaven. As Paul says, "Eye has not seen, nor ear heard, nor have entered into

> The rewards for walking with God and doing His will are going to be better than anything we can imagine, and they will last forever.

the heart of man the things which God has prepared for those who love Him."[1] The rewards for walking with God and doing His will are going to be better than anything we can imagine, and they will last forever.

It starts at the cross

In the beginning of this book, we looked at how knowing God's will starts at the Cross. You and I were separated from God by our sins. Jesus' death on the cross reconciled us to God. There would be no

---

[1] 1 Corinthians 2:9

relationship with God and no walking in His will, if it weren't for Jesus dying on the cross. As Jesus said, "No one comes to the Father except through Me."[2] The cross is the means to knowing the will of God.

It continues at the cross

The cross is also the motivation for doing the will of God. When we look at what Jesus did for us on the cross, we see just how much God loves us. He loves us with an everlasting love and He has plans for your life and mine- perfect plans. Our reasonable response is to want to do His will.

Jesus said, "If anyone desires to come after Me, let him deny himself, and take up his cross daily, and follow Me."[3] Knowing the will of God involves you and me taking up our crosses to follow Jesus. "Taking up your cross" is self-denial. It is saying, "I am willing to die to my desires, plans, possessions and dreams in order to please and follow the One who gave His life for me." It is saying, "I surrender all, I surrender all. All to Jesus I surrender, I surrender all."

> **Through His cross, we are reconciled to God and motivated to live for Him. Through our cross, we become like Jesus- we offer our life to God and we allow Him to guide us into His perfect will.**

Knowing the will of God, starts, continues, and ends at the cross. Through His cross, we are reconciled to God and motivated to live for

---

[2] John 14:6
[3] Luke 9:23

Him. Through our cross, we become like Jesus- we offer our life to God and we allow Him to guide us into His perfect will.

It ends at the cross

There is nothing more beautiful in the human experience than a Christ-like life- a surrendered life, a life that pleases and brings glory to God; when we, on a daily basis, say in effect, "Lord, You alone are worthy. I love you and I want to do your will." We offer God the clay pot of our self and He fills us with the Wonderful Spirit of Himself.

There is a tremendous sense of peace and contentment in knowing that you are right where God wants you to be, doing what God wants you to be doing. No matter what you are going through, you can know that God is with you and that He is for you. You can have His peace and joy every day.

It will also be wonderful at the end of your life, to be able, like Paul, to say, "I have fought the good fight, I have finished the race, I have kept the faith."[4] And to know that one day, you will stand before Him and He will say to you, "Well done," and welcome you into His presence, into His joy- fullness of joy. It will be a day that is better than any day you can imagine. It will be joy unspeakable. And it will last forever. God loves you, His plans for you are good, and He wants you to know His perfect will for your life.

---

[4] 2 Timothy 4:7-8

As you seek to live a life of knowing the will of God, I pray that you will know God in a deeper and richer way than you have ever imagined. I pray that "the God of our Lord Jesus Christ, the Father of glory, may give to you the spirit of wisdom and revelation in the knowledge of Him, the eyes of your understanding being enlightened; that you may know what is the hope of His calling, what are the riches of the glory of His inheritance in the saints, and what is the exceeding greatness of His power toward us who believe, according to the working of His mighty power." [5] *and you will "stand perfect and complete in all the will of God."* [6] *Lastly, I pray that you will know God's will for your life-every day.*

For a soon-coming Free study guide to this book, check out- www.howtoknowthewillofGod.com

If this book has been a blessing to you, I'd love to hear about it- strat@howtoknowthewillofGod.com

---

[5] Ephesians 1:17-19
[6] Colossians 4:12

How to know the will of God

C. - Commit

Commit yourself to God, to prayer, and to knowing and doing God's will.

R. - Read

God speaks through His Word. Read God's Word regularly (meditate on it and memorize it).

-What does God's Word say?
-What is God saying specifically to you?

O. - Observe

God speaks through circumstances. Look around and see what seems like the good thing to do.

S. - Still, small voice

God speaks to His people. Often it's through His still, small voice.

S. - Saints

God speaks through His people. Listen to the counsel of godly believers.

Scriptures for meditation and prayer-

"...neither death nor life, nor angels nor principalities nor powers, nor things present nor things to come, nor height nor depth, nor any other created thing, shall be able to separate us from the love of God which is in Christ Jesus our Lord."   - Romans 8:38-39

"I beseech you therefore, brethren, by the mercies of God, that you present your bodies a living sacrifice, holy, acceptable to God, which is your reasonable service. And do not be conformed to this world, but be transformed by the renewing of your mind, that you may prove what is that good and acceptable and perfect will of God."   - Romans 12:1-2

"Trust in the LORD with all your heart, and lean not on your own understanding; In all your ways acknowledge Him, And He shall direct your paths."
                                           - Proverbs 3:5,6

"As for God, His way is perfect; The word of the LORD is proven; He is a shield to all who trust in Him... It is God who arms me with strength, and makes my way perfect."   - Psalm 18:30, 32

"But as it is written: 'Eye has not seen, nor ear heard, nor have entered into the heart of man the things which God has prepared for those who love Him.'"
                                        - 1 Corinthians 2:9

"We love Him because He first loved us." - 1 John 4:19

"...they shall call His name Immanuel, which is translated, 'God with us'"   - Matthew 1:23

"...The LORD will guide you continually..."
- Isaiah 58:11

"Your word is a lamp to my feet and a light to my path."   - Psalm 119:105

"And let the peace of God rule in your hearts, to which also you were called in one body; and be thankful."
- Colossians 3:15

"...for it is God who works in you both to will and to do for His good pleasure."   - Phillippians 2:13

"Then Jesus spoke to them again, saying, 'I am the light of the world. He who follows Me shall not walk in darkness, but have the light of life.'"   - John 8:12

"You will show me the path of life; In Your presence is fullness of joy; At Your right hand are pleasures forevermore."   - Psalm 16:11

"Therefore do not be unwise, but understand what the will of the Lord is."   - Ephesians 5:17

"For He Himself has said, 'I will never leave you nor forsake you.'"   - Hebrews 13:5

"If any of you lacks wisdom, let him ask of God, who gives to all liberally and without reproach, and it will be given to him."   - James 1:5

"His lord said to him, 'Well done, good and faithful servant; you have been faithful over a few things, I will make you ruler over many things. Enter into the joy of your lord.'"   - Matthew 25:23

"... as bondservants of Christ, doing the will of God from the heart..."   - Ephesians 6:6

"Rejoice always, pray without ceasing, in everything give thanks; for this is the will of God in Christ Jesus for you."   - 1 Thessalonian 5:16-18

"I will instruct you and teach you in the way you should go; I will guide you with My eye." - Psalm 32:8

"Obey My voice, and I will be your God, and you shall be My people. And walk in all the ways that I have commanded you, that it may be well with you."
                    - Jeremiah 7:23

"...whoever listens to Me will dwell safely, and will be secure, without fear of evil."   - Proverbs 1:33

"...always laboring fervently for you in prayers, that you may stand perfect and complete in all the will of God."   - Colossians 4:12

"...and the sheep hear his voice; and he calls his own sheep by name and leads them out. And when he brings out his own sheep, he goes before them; and the sheep follow him, for they know his voice."
                    - John 10:3-4

"Now may the God of peace who brought up our Lord Jesus from the dead, that great Shepherd of the sheep, through the blood of the everlasting covenant, make you complete in every good work to do His will, working in you what is well pleasing in His sight, through Jesus Christ, to whom be glory forever and ever. Amen."   - Hebrews 13:20-21

QUICK ORDER FORM

⌨ **Email orders:** orders@firstcallpublishing.org

☎ **Order by phone:** 800-456-2421 (Toll free)

    ☎ From Hawaii- 808-214-5184

    Please have your credit card ready.

▤ **Fax orders:** 800-456-2421. Please send this form.

▣ **Order by mail:**

    First Call Publishing, P.O. BOX 81459, Haiku, HI 96708, USA

Please send _____ copies of the book How to Know the Will of God.
(Please include payment.)

Please send me (free) information on:

    ☐ Future Books and Study Guides by Strat Goodhue
    ☐ Speaking/Conferences/ Retreats
    ☐ Put me on your email/mailing list

Name: _____

Address: _____

City: _____ State: _____ Zip:_____

Telephone: _____

Email address: _____

Prices- Go to- www.howtoknowthewillofGod.com for lower prices.

Number of books	Price per book	Shipping
1	$12.00	$4.00
2-3	$9.60	$5.15
4-20	$8.40	$11.35
21-27	$7.20	$15.35

28 or more- Please call or email for pricing

Excise Tax: Please add 4% for books shipped to Hawaii addresses.

International Shipping: $9.00 for first book, $5.00 for each additional.

God bless you as you seek Him.